"When Christian authors of late anti‥ ⸻ has
to do with matters of doctrine, like t ⸻ :flec-
tions on the Trinity, for instance. Bu. ⸻ :ship,
and soul care are also of immense value for our day. To be ‥⸺ world
quite different from ours in all kinds of ways. However, such basic issues as human
pride, abuse of power, and sexual lust were as common in their world as they are in
ours. And their wisdom on how to deal with these matters as well as their pungent
and powerful reflections on spiritual formation are of enormous value in our bent
world. This is a book to be read slowly and treasured."

Michael A. G. Haykin, Professor of Church History and Biblical
Spirituality, The Southern Baptist Theological Seminary

"*Ancient Wisdom for the Care of Souls* is a brilliantly conceived volume, weaving together
faithful biblical interpretation, engaging historical theology, thoughtful spiritual formation, and practical pastoral care as seen through the window of the church fathers
and classical Trinitarian thought. It draws from the rich tradition of the church's early
centuries and provides pastors, students, and church leaders examples of great wisdom
for the rigorous and complex challenges of ministry in our contemporary context. This
book offers insights regarding the virtue, spirituality, theological depth, and ministry
skills needed in those charged with the responsibility of spiritual oversight and the
care of souls. Three cheers for Coleman Ford and Shawn Wilhite for writing this
wonderful book, which will serve as a treasured resource for many for years to come."

David S. Dockery, President and Distinguished Professor of Theology,
Southwestern Baptist Theological Seminary; President, International
Alliance for Christian Education

"Pastoral ministry lies at the heart of the church. Its outward form is constantly
changing, but its underlying principles remain the same. The distilled wisdom of the
past is an encouragement in the present, as this guide to the teaching and practice
of great leaders of the early church makes plain. It is a precious resource for us to
ponder and to use in our service to the Lord today."

Gerald Bray, Research Professor, Beeson Divinity School

"Sometimes it takes getting out of our own culture to see our misguided assumptions, including those about ministry. As pastors, we need to prioritize Scripture as
our authority and glean wisdom from the local church, the global church, and the
historic church. This helpful volume takes us back to the early church so we can learn
from the church fathers about pastoral spirituality, theology, and ministry."

Christopher W. Morgan, Dean, School of Christian Ministries, California
Baptist University; Pastor, Immanuel Baptist Church, Highland, California

Ancient Wisdom for the Care of Souls

Ancient Wisdom for the Care of Souls

Learning the Art of Pastoral Ministry
from the Church Fathers

Coleman M. Ford and Shawn J. Wilhite

Foreword by Ray Ortlund

WHEATON, ILLINOIS

Library of Congress Cataloging-in-Publication Data

Names: Ford, Coleman M., author. | Wilhite, Shawn J., author.
Title: Ancient wisdom for the care of souls : learning the art of pastoral ministry from the church fathers / Coleman M. Ford and Shawn J. Wilhite.
Description: Wheaton, Illinois : Crossway, 2024. | Includes bibliographical references and index.
Identifiers: LCCN 2023049144 (print) | LCCN 2023049145 (ebook) | ISBN 9781433575495 (trade paperback) | ISBN 9781433575501 (pdf) | ISBN 9781433575525 (epub)
Subjects: LCSH: Church work. | Christian literature, Early.
Classification: LCC BV4400 .F63 2024 (print) | LCC BV4400 (ebook) | DDC 253–dc23/eng/20240213
LC record available at https://lccn.loc.gov/2023049144
LC ebook record available at https://lccn.loc.gov/2023049145

For the elders, deacons, and ministry staff of the Village Church Denton,
who are a beautiful model of Christ's humility and abundant grace.
Coleman

For the elders, deacons, and ministry staff of Redeemer
Baptist Church. It fills me with exceeding joy to labor
alongside each of you for the joy of the bride.
Shawn

Contents

Foreword

WHEN WE CHRISTIANS recite the Apostles' Creed in our worship services, we affirm not only "the holy catholic church" but also "the communion of saints."[1] These two articles of faith are related, of course, but they are not identical. The holy catholic church is the whole body of people throughout time, anywhere and everywhere, who have believed in the Lord Jesus Christ. The communion of saints is the ongoing fellowship and solidarity among those believers in Christ. It's their shared life together. The first is an entity, the second an experience.

The communion of saints is one reason why this book matters. Our sympathies flow out toward the whole church. Yes, we are compelled by history and geography to gather together in local churches, which might appear more like separation than communion. But in our hearts, we cherish, we affirm, we revere the communion of saints as a grace from our Savior God (Eph. 4:4–6; Heb. 12:22–24).

---

1   Chad Van Dixhoorn, ed., *Creeds, Confessions, and Catechisms: A Reader's Edition* (Wheaton, IL: Crossway, 2022), 13.

So, then, we have an answer to the question, Why go back to the patristic era for pastoral wisdom today? The answer is, we today are located *within* the ancient, medieval, and modern communion of saints! We should instead ask, Why *not* go back?

Our pastoral resources are not limited to our time. We have helps for our generation from beyond our generation. Let's not leap mentally from the apostles of the first century to the Reformers of the sixteenth century, as if God's people in the intervening centuries had nothing to say. Thomas Cranmer, the English Reformer, believed that the church had lost its way only in the three or four centuries prior to his own time. He believed that, in going so wrong, the church had departed not only from the Scriptures but also from the fathers.[2] Let's take full advantage of the profound resources God has provided for us today in those saints then!

Coleman Ford and Shawn Wilhite's new book, *Ancient Wisdom for the Care of Souls: Learning the Art of Pastoral Ministry from the Church Fathers*, opens a door for our generation of pastors to be enriched by this ancient wisdom. It's as if a circle of elderly pastors from those centuries long ago is standing together, discussing pastoral ministry, each one contributing his own experience and insights. Ford and Wilhite are over here, standing with us, pointing to them over there and saying, "Those saints aren't all that far away. Just a few steps. And we could learn from them. Want to walk over and listen in for a while?" Who would refuse such an offer?

Thank you, Coleman and Shawn, for helping us get free of the narrow limits of our time. We're tired of hype and celebrity. We

2 J. I. Packer, "Introduction," in *The Work of Thomas Cranmer*, ed. G. E. Duffield (Philadelphia: Fortress, 1965), xi–xiii.

long for gospel ministry that's been time-tested, that's real and solid and lasting. Thank you for showing us a path into the communion of saints deeper and richer than we have known thus far—and all by God's grace alone, for his glory alone.

Ray Ortlund
RENEWAL MINISTRIES

Acknowledgments

WE HAVE BEEN FRIENDS for the better part of twelve years, and our friendship forged this book. The topics of our text threads and conversations range from music interests to patristics, pictures of books, praying for one another, and caring for our families. We have decided to write this book because of our mutual interest in ministry and patristics, but it also affords us even more ways to explore the depth of our friendship.

No book is ever written without the influences (living or dead) that surround an author. I (Coleman) wish to thank many mentors who have shaped my thinking and ministry throughout the years. Jerry Witham was the first true pastor I had, modeling the work of pastoral ministry and providing me with opportunities to grow and develop as a preacher and minister of the gospel. Michael Haykin showed me what it means to receive the voices of tradition with grace and charity. I am thankful to the many fellow ministers of the gospel, both past and present, with whom I have had the pleasure of serving alongside. You all demonstrate the heart of a pastor and have shaped and encouraged me in myriad ways. Alex, my wife and partner in ministry, has greatly encouraged me in my ministry calling and writing. The Fordlings

(Colette, Matthieu, and Charlotte) bring so much joy to me along the way. Thank you all!

I (Shawn) wish to express gratitude and thanks for several mentors and spiritual directors: Greg Cochran and Jeff Mooney for modeling a patient and caring ministry to the church, Michael Haykin and Lewis Ayres for teaching me how to read the fathers slowly and patiently, and Jeff Biddle for showing me how to care for souls. I also wish to thank my students at California Baptist University (CBU) and Gateway Seminary as well as the ministry interns at Redeemer (especially Matt, who began as an intern, became one of my disciples, and now serves as my pastor). I am incredibly grateful to belong to Redeemer and CBU. My deans, Chris Morgan and Tony Chute, have greatly supported me and my research interests. My partner and co-heir in this life, Allyson, and my beloved kiddies (Mercy and Caden) have added value to my life in ways unimaginable. Thanks to each of you.

We cannot accept full credit for the final outcome of this book. We are incredibly thankful to the wonderful team at Crossway, including Todd Augustine for shepherding this project with us and especially Jenny-Lyn de Klerk for her keen editorial insight. Her tireless work and dedication contributed immensely to what you hold in your hands. Her polishing is invisibly present all throughout and we would be negligent in not thanking her for her incredible work. Of course, any errors that remain fall squarely on our own shoulders.

Last we are deeply indebted to and grateful for the Christian sisters and brothers in our lives. The normal and ordinary relationships we experience week in and week out at the Village Church Denton and Redeemer Baptist Church continue to shape our spiritual lives and how we minister to others. It is to the pastors, deacons, and ministry servants of these churches that we dedicate this book. May you live a life of slowness, virtue, patience, and joy as you shepherd the church among you.

Coleman M. Ford and Shawn J. Wilhite
PASCHAL TRIDIUM 2023

Introduction

The Contemporary Pastor and the Classical Tradition

I (SHAWN) REMEMBER THE FIRST TIME that a local church's philosophy of ministry collided with my vision of theology. I was an associate pastor at the time and it was a surreal moment as I realized how many cultural assumptions in this local church did not match my evolving theological vision. During this season, I was unaware of the classical tradition of the church.[1] Unable to change the culture of this local setting, I became quite discouraged—jaded in many ways. I settled for a less-than-ideal church culture and resolved to live with my pastoral and theological idealism.

On another occasion, I remember walking down the hall of an emergency room to visit a church member. She had been recently admitted and was hooked up to a ventilator by the time I arrived. These machines essentially enabled her body to remain functioning

---

1   See Andrew Purves, *Pastoral Theology in the Classical Tradition* (Louisville, KY: Westminster John Knox, 2001). In our book, "classical tradition" refers to the writings and visual culture of the church before the modern era that affirmed the ecumenical creeds.

for hours. We later discovered that she had a stroke earlier in the morning and presumably died at that moment but had been revived. Several friends and church members would come throughout the day to kiss her forehead, whisper in her ear, and mourn at her feet. Merely two weeks before her death, I visited her in the hospital, where she recounted how the gospel had transformed her life. As I sat near her while she lay dying in her hospital bed, I was reminded of two different realities: the beauty of Jesus's work of transforming lives and the burdens of pastoral ministry. That day, her pastors and friends from our church family sang hymns around her bedside (written hundreds of years before this very moment), prayed for her, and read Scripture with her as she slowly passed from this life into the presence of Jesus.

These stories highlight a certain tension within pastoral ministry: how does a theological vision shape pastoral ministry? The complexities of Christian theology ought to be reflected in the cultural life of the local church and the shepherding duties of its pastors. But a quick glance at local churches and denominational structures may reveal a host of problems—abuses of leadership, an inappropriate adoption of CEO models, minimizing theological depth in the name of reaching the lost, a diminishing value of church membership, confusion regarding the qualifications and role of a pastor, and much more. It takes a skilled and winsome pastor to observe and speak into these patterns and present a rich vision of Christian theology for the church.

Coleman and I are quite happy to watch a philosophical shift toward older traditions within the Protestant landscape as believers feel disillusioned with modern models of ministry. As several Christian thinkers focus on classical traditions, a *ressourcement*—that is, a mode of theology that listens to voices from different eras in order to learn from, be shaped by, and resource them for modern expression—is occurring within the Protestant theological culture.[2] Henri de Lubac, a French Jesuit in the twentieth century, said, "Every time, in the West, that Christian renewal has flourished, in the order of thought and that of life . . . it has flourished under the sign of the Fathers."[3] We hope the resurgence of classical traditions is not a fad but a true recovery of spiritual and theological vitality for the modern church. We hope patristic and medieval *ressourcement* is more than a growing trend and serves as the philosophical and theological medicine that will help cure shallow evangelical practice.

Though Christians pursue formal and informal theological training to serve local churches, we are aware that pastors are neck-deep in the throes of pastoral ministry. We also understand that burnout in pastoral ministry is a real and present danger. Often it comes about when we are operating at a spiritual deficit rather than surplus. Pete Scazzero observes that "spiritual deficits typically reveal themselves in too much activity. Unhealthy leaders engage in more activities than their combined spiritual, physical, and emotional reserves can sustain."[4] As budgets need to be met and attendance numbers need to grow, pastors may be tempted to explore ministry gimmicks or shortcuts to meet these practical concerns. But what you use to win people, you will probably use to retain people. If

2 See Michael Allen and Scott R. Swain, *Reformed Catholicity: The Promise of Retrieval for Theology and Biblical Interpretation* (Grand Rapids, MI: Baker Academic, 2015) and John Webster, *The Culture of Theology*, ed. Ivor J. Davidson and Alden C. McCray (Grand Rapids, MI: Baker Academic, 2019).

3 Henri de Lubac, *At the Service of the Church: Henri de Lubac Reflects on the Circumstances That Occasioned His Writings* (San Francisco, CA: Ignatius, 1992), 317–18.

4 Peter Scazzero, *The Emotionally Healthy Leader: How Transforming Your Inner Life Will Deeply Transform Your Church, Team, and the World* (Grand Rapids, MI: Zondervan, 2015), 26.

we primarily entertain churchgoers, we will need to continue entertaining in order to keep them around.

Coleman and I believe that ministers should instead use the depth of the Scriptures, a vision of the Trinitarian God, and wisdom from the classical traditions as the foundation of local and global ministry. Pastors should help people see the beauties of God as displayed in Scripture and active in the life of the historic church and show them how the triune God is the source of all things and how the ancient creeds of the church tether us to an orthodox vision of God. These three anchors—Scripture, Trinitarian theology, and church history—stabilize the church's moorings in an ever-shifting world. We echo what Trevin Wax has observed:

> The ancient Christians worked for decades on arriving at a place of clarity concerning the nature of Christ's identity, not because they were obsessed with the smallest of details or had a propensity toward theological wrangling, but because they knew orthodoxy wasn't some dry, abstract definition—it was a portrait of a real and living God.[5]

Pastors and their people must dwell in the life of God for the good of their souls and the good of the world.

As we watch the modern and late-modern experiments fail to satisfy our souls, we believe the recovery of classic Christian traditions should increase. According to L. O. Mills, "the history of pastoral care is largely unclaimed and unknown" today.[6] Additionally,

---

5 Trevin Wax, *The Thrill of Orthodoxy: Rediscovering the Adventure of Christian Faith* (Downers Grove, IL: Intervarsity, 2022), 43.

6 L. O. Mills, "Pastoral Care (History, Traditions, and Definitions)," in *Dictionary of Pastoral Care and Counseling*, ed. Rodney J. Hunter (Nashville, TN: Abingdon, 1990), 836.

Andrew Purves suggests, "Contemporary pastoral care is, by and large, uninformed by historical practice."[7] As a result, pastors are not taught what the church's theological heritage says about pastoral ministry.[8] But this heritage has much to teach us.

Discovering a Classical Vision of Pastoral Ministry

Early in ministry, Shawn and I often heard, "The pastor is supposed to do such and such" regarding various extrabiblical tasks. Several people had expectations that were not rooted in a biblical vision of the pastoral office. It certainly took time for us to learn (and continue to learn) how to remain teachable to some and lead others toward a biblical vision of the pastoral office. But, in general, too many items have been added to the pastor's job description. According to Scripture, the pastor first and foremost prays (Acts 6), shepherds his people (1 Pet. 5), lives a virtuous life in the Spirit, and upholds sound teaching in local settings.

While writing this chapter, I (Coleman) overheard two women describing their church experiences over the last few years. One heard a feel-good message and was then herded out of the sanctuary; she did not feel known or seen. The other said she wanted to be in a church that was more rooted in the community. Both were expressing the desire to attend church in the town where they live, be integrated with others in the community, and be known by their church family and its leaders. This casual conversation in a suburban

---

7 Purves, *Pastoral Theology in the Classical Tradition*, 5.

8 Thomas C. Oden, *Pastoral Theology: Essentials of Ministry* (New York: Harper Collins, 1983); Thomas C. Oden, *Care of the Souls in the Classical Tradition* (Minneapolis, MN: Fortress, 1984); Alastair V. Campbell, *Rediscovering Pastoral Care* (London: Darton, Longman, and Todd, 1986); Eugene Peterson, *Five Smooth Stones for Pastoral Work* (Grand Rapids, MI: Eerdmans, 1992); Michael A. G. Haykin, Brian Croft, and Ian H. Clary, *Being a Pastor: A Conversation with Andrew Fuller* (Durham: Evangelical, 2019).

coffee shop in north Texas over iced lattes perfectly represents why we wrote this book. While we don't want to idolize a specific vision of church life, we do want to bring the ancient voices of the church fathers to bear on this topic. We offer a simple vision of a pastor who prays, tends to people's souls, and preaches the life-giving word of God. This kind of pastor pursues virtue, contemplation, and slowness. He equips the church and shepherds people's souls. He cultivates communal and individual liturgies. He leads a local church that, though unknown to the rest of the world, is vital to the surrounding neighborhoods. Overall, the classical pastor is the quiet pastor who displays a peaceful temperament and ministers to souls in his local setting.[9]

In order to do this, the classical pastor contemplates and proclaims the beauties of the triune God, the gospel, and the Scriptures, using this to walk with people through their current life into the next. He takes these beauties and shows people how to find joy and happiness in God during this life. In a single day, he may walk with someone who shared the gospel for the first time, someone who criticizes his last sermon, someone whose marriage he officiated but who is now on the verge of divorce, and someone expressing an interest in missions work. Such pastors administer the riches of

---

9   This is not to say that humble pastors will not be noticed or lauded by others but that they do not seek acclaim in their pastoral ministry. A recent example of such a pastor is Timothy Keller. While well-known and widely published, all accounts show him as a humble and well-tempered man who cared about the souls to whom he ministered. For more on the life and pastoral ministry of Tim Keller see Collin Hansen, *Timothy Keller: His Spiritual and Intellectual Formation* (Grand Rapids, MI: Zondervan, 2023). Another example is Eugene Peterson, well-known author of *The Message* and numerous books on Christian living, who produced his works with his local congregation in mind. Notoriety was not his goal but was a by-product of his faithfulness to ministry. For more on his pastoral ministry see Eugene H. Peterson, *The Pastor: A Memoir* (New York: HarperOne, 2012) and Will Collier, *A Burning in My Bones: The Authorized Biography of Eugene H. Peterson* (Colorado Springs: Waterbrook, 2022).

God to address the complexities of various situations in his congregants' lives, model godly living, and equip others for ministry. Navigating this pastoral life is, as the fathers said, the "art of arts."[10]

More precisely, a classical vision for ministry is characterized by the following marks:

1. Classical theology: classical pastoral ministry confesses a theology that rests on the historic confessions of the church—including the three Western creeds (the Nicene, Athanasian, and Apostles' creeds) and the Chalcedonian Definition—and is informed by the church fathers.

2. Virtue: classical pastoral ministry holds in high regard the health of the church—especially for the purpose of theological clarity and spiritual care—and this is seen in the flourishing of Christian virtues. Further, the primary qualifications for a pastor are these virtues.

3. Integrated spirituality and theology: classical pastoral ministry places no unneeded dichotomy between theological study and spiritual feeling. In other words, classical pastors think deeply about the divine mysteries and personally experience them.

4. Local community: classical pastoral ministry offers pastoral theology and care within the locus of the local church, and

---

10 This phrase is taken from Gregory the Great: "No one presumes to teach an art that he has not first mastered through study. How foolish it is therefore for the inexperienced to assume pastoral authority when the care of souls is the art of arts." St. Gregory the Great, *The Book of Pastoral Rule*, trans. George E. Demacopoulos, Popular Patristics Series 34 (Crestwood, NY: St. Vladimir's Seminary Press, 2007), pt. 1, sec. 1. Similarly, Gregory of Nazianzus called soul care the "art of arts and science of sciences." Gregory of Nazianzus, *Oration 2*, in *Nicene and Post-Nicene Fathers, Second Series*, trans. Charles Gordon Browne and James Edward Swallow (Peabody, MA: Hendrickson, 1994), 7:208.

this then spills outward to the wider church for its benefit
(not vice versa).

5. Care of souls: classical pastoral ministry is a ministry of
soul care—for both ministers and the congregation. Care,
or curing, of souls is using biblical wisdom to bring true,
sustained, and holistic health to the life of the church.

In addition to these marks, we can also identify a main guiding
principle of classical vision for pastoral ministry, namely, what
the fathers called the "double love," or love of God and neighbor
according to Matthew 22:37–40. Here, Jesus said, "You shall love
the Lord your God with all your heart and with all your soul and
with all your mind. This is the great and first commandment. And
a second is like it: You shall love your neighbor as yourself. On
these two commandments depend all the Law and the Prophets."

In the pastoral office, to love God is to thoughtfully and prayerfully commune with God, to contemplate and spend time with
him. This activity cannot be measured on a chart and is rarely seen
by others. To love one's neighbor is to thoughtfully and prayerfully
connect with people in one's congregation and community through
preaching, soul care, discipleship, evangelism, and presence. These
activities can be measured but not necessarily the results.

Thus, in this classical vision for pastoral ministry, depth of theology and care of souls go hand in hand. Defining theology as a purely
intellectual enterprise betrays a misunderstanding of theology alto-
gether. And pursuing soul care apart from a deep well of theology
leads to dry human pursuits with parched human solutions. Instead,
we must drink from the deepest well of contemplative theology to
minister to all those who are thirsty. Early Christian pastors dug
a deep well of theology to bring forth water for the care of souls,

and we can glean many insights from this tradition that will help us deepen our ministry, enrich our theological reflection, and vivify our spiritual communion with God. This book will help you dig that well afresh (or anew).

Corrections to Pastoral Ministry in Our Modern World

Overall, recovering this classical vision of pastoral ministry can help us correct three misunderstandings regarding the nature of ministry today. First, the role of the pastor is not to serve as a CEO of a business but to walk the neighborhoods and visit the homes of Christians. We realize that a local gathering of believers must pay rent for a building and process weekly, monthly, and yearly expenditures—many items that require business skills. But we must resist the temptation to allow the church's business to override the pastoral functions. Pastors are not just the holy CEO charged with keeping the doors open and the church budget in the black—they must concern themselves with souls.

Second, the role of the pastor is not to meet a quota of souls who attend services but to provide care for souls. Faithful pastoral ministry may translate into more people in the pew, but it is not the decisive factor. We know many faithful churches that have hundreds and thousands of members shepherded by godly ministers. We also know faithful pastors who shepherd just a few dozen souls. And though an evangelistic culture in the church is a good thing, it's not good when pursued at the expense of deep formation and theological precision. So how can we recover the model of local pastors who are known deeply by their local community, whether in a small country parish or a larger suburban church? A single pastor can efficiently and faithfully shepherd, at most, fifty to eighty people. If a local church is home to five hundred members, then that local body of Christians may need at least ten elders to shepherd each person well (a 1:50 ratio). Pragmatism often impedes such a vision, but pastoral ministry is about shepherding people—full stop. Church elders must have time and space to get to know people and care for their souls.

Finally, the role of the pastor is not to make decisions primarily on the basis of what is convenient but what is theologically true. I (Shawn) remember a pastor saying, "I have preached expositionally through Hebrews for a full year, and it didn't work,"[11] and Coleman remembers planning a meeting where someone advocated for adding a Saturday evening service to accommodate families and young adults. Such comments reveal pragmatic commitments. We understand the need to serve our people and address the effectiveness of our preaching and teaching, but we believe local pastors must maintain a clear theological vision that upholds doctrine and pursues deep theology for the church's health.[12] We do not do things primarily because they produce certain results; we do things because we are convinced they are based on good theology and because they are the best things to do for the souls in our congregation.

Looking Backward to Move Forward

As previously stated, this book is one of *ressourcement*. Another word for this is retrieval. According to John Webster, "The major achievements of theology in the mode of retrieval have been to commend a more celebratory style of theological portrayal and to

---

11 All quotations that do not list a source are taken from the authors' personal experiences.

12 We agree with the pastor-theologian model proposed (or perhaps recovered) in Gerald Hiestand and Todd Wilson, *The Pastor Theologian: Resurrecting an Ancient Vision* (Grand Rapids, MI: Zondervan, 2015).

rehabilitate classical sources of Christian teaching and draw attention to their potential in furthering the theological task."[13] Patristic studies have rightly influenced modern hermeneutical theory, Trinitarian doctrine, and selected studies of Christian spirituality.[14] We aim to continue this trajectory of patristic *ressourcement* with an eye toward pastoral ministry.

Todd Billings posits, "If the idea of reading very old commentaries on Scripture is new to you, it may seem counterintuitive. Aren't we supposed to interpret the Bible as God's word for *today*?"[15] This question frequently enters the pastor's study as he prepares to say something meaningful about his people's struggles.[16] Why would we consider reading something antiquarian to address modern concerns? For some, the ancient authors seem odd, and so do their interpretations of Scripture. For others, what these authors wrote about seems irrelevant to the modern issues pastors need to address today.

But it is precisely by retrieving these sources that pastors can most effectively minister to their people. Timothy George, a theologian

---

13 John Webster, "Theologies of Retrieval," in *The Oxford Handbook of Systematic Theology*, ed. John Webster, Kathryn Tanner, and Ian Torrance (Oxford: Oxford University Press, 2009), 596.

14 John J. O'Keefe and Russell R. Reno, *Sanctified Vision: An Introduction to Early Christian Interpretation of the Bible* (Baltimore, MD: John Hopkins University Press, 2005); Peter Sanlon, *Simply God: Recovering the Classical Trinity* (Nottingham: Inter-Varsity, 2014); Fred Sanders, *The Triune God*, New Studies in Dogmatics (Grand Rapids, MI: Zondervan, 2016); Shawn J. Wilhite "Spirituality in the Patristic Era," in *Early Christian Doctrine*, ed. Michael A. G. Haykin and Michael Strickland (Bellingham, WA: Lexham, forthcoming); Coleman M. Ford, *Formed in His Image: A Guide for Christian Formation* (Nashville, TN: B&H, 2023).

15 J. Todd Billings, *The Word of God for the People of God: An Entryway to the Theological Interpretation of Scripture* (Grand Rapids, MI: Eerdmans, 2010), 151.

16 The rest of this section has been adapted from Shawn J. Wilhite, "Integrating Patristic Voices in the Local Church," The Center for Baptist Renewal, April 17, 2018, https://www.center forbaptistrenewal.com/. Used by permission.

and church historian, has brilliantly referred to this kind of retrieval as "retrieval for the sake of renewal."[17] He explains,

> What is retrieval? It is not just refurbishment. It is not just going back and finding something or someone famous four or five hundred years ago and dusting them off and letting them shine again in all of their glory. There is nothing wrong with that, but more is involved in retrieval. *Retrieval is more of a rescue operation.* It recognizes that there is a great deal of our Christian past that has become obscure, that we just don't know about anymore. Retrieval looks at these figures as our fellow sojourners in the life of faith. We are one with them in Jesus Christ. They are guiding lights for the people of God throughout the ages. That sometimes means we have to ask new and different questions of them, different from what they were asking in their own day. We have the right, and even the responsibility, to do just that.[18]

Michael Allen explains this kind of retrieval using archeology as an illustration, saying that when we dig deep into the tradition of our heritage, we discover the well and repository of the satisfying riches in Christ and his bride.[19] Rowan Williams thus calls theological retrieval "creative archaeology."[20]

This does not mean that theological retrieval is an uncritical acceptance of ancient readings of the Bible or theological affirmations,

---

17 Timothy George, "Retrieval for the Sake of Renewal," *Reformed Faith & Practice* 2, no. 2 (2017).

18 George, "Retrieval for the Sake of Renewal," 73.

19 Michael Allen, "Reformed Retrieval," in *Theology of Retrieval: An Exploration and Appraisal*, ed. Darren Sarisky, T&T Clark Theology (London: Bloomsbury, 2019), 67–68.

20 Rowan Williams, *Why Study the Past? The Quest for the Historical Church* (London: Darton, Longman, and Todd, 2005), 100.

a prioritizing of older voices over newer voices, or a rejection of modern methods of Bible interpretation.[21] It is good and right to analyze writings from the past, and, as people living in the twenty-first century, pastors cannot ignore modern scholarship on the Bible.

Rather, theological retrieval is excavating the past and allowing ancient sources to influence and contribute to modern ideas. It assumes that doing theology is studying God and all other things in relation to God, including the past. Our theological progress is incomplete but arriving at greater and greater clarity as the church continually engages with the Scriptures, the culture it lives in, and the tradition it has received. This process helps us to consider texts critically and diligently as we mine the Christian tradition, recover its valuable features, and use all the riches of the Spirit's work in the church, including those from history. Billings helps us bring all of these ideas together when he says,

> In the end, we should read premodern exegetes in particular not because we always agree with their positions. Indeed, they often disagree with each other. We should not read them because they replace or make obsolete the insights that come from critical studies of the Bible. Premodern interpreters are fallible and limited, as are we. But they also reflect the work of the Spirit in the past, and they show great insight into how to interpret all of Scripture as God's own word in Christ.[22]

---

21 " 'Retrieval', then, is a *mode* of theology, an attitude of mind and a way of approaching theological tasks which is present with greater or lesser prominence in a range of different thinkers, not all of them self-consciously 'conservative' or 'orthodox.' " John Webster, "Theologies of Retrieval," in *The Oxford Handbook of Systematic Theology*, ed. John Webster, Kathryn Tanner, and Ian Torrance (Oxford: Oxford University Press, 2009), 584.

22 Billings, *Word of God for the People of God*, 188.

Thus, in the spirit of renewal or *ressourcement*, each chapter of this book will seek to learn from a particular church father regarding (1) the virtues and spiritual life of a pastor, (2) the theological vision of a pastor, or (3) the ministry of a pastor. As you read, we hope these facets will come together to provide a holistic picture of classical pastoral ministry. Only a few pastoral treatises exist in the patristic tradition—Gregory of Nazianzus's *In Defense of His Flight to Pontus*, John Chrysostom's *On the Priesthood*, Ambrose of Milan's *On the Duties of the Clergy*, and Gregory the Great's *Pastoral Rule*. We will interact with each of these in various chapters throughout the book.

In addition to this, we will also consider some important Scripture texts on pastoral ministry and reflect on our ministerial experience. As Protestants, we view Scripture, tradition, and experience as helpful aids to uncovering truth. Though the tradition examined in this book—the church fathers—is not on the same level as Scripture, we desire to listen attentively to their wisdom.[23] John Jewel (1522–1571) highlighted what we aim to follow:

> But what say we of the fathers, Augustine, Ambrose, Jerome, Cyprian, etc.? What shall we think of them, or what account may we make of them? They be interpreters of the word of God. They were learned men, and learned fathers; the instruments of mercy of God, and vessels full of grace. We despise them not, we read them, we reverence them, and give thanks unto God for them. They were witnesses unto the truth, they were worthy

---

23 "The Fathers are not Scripture. They are senior conversation partners about Scripture and its meaning. We listen to them respectfully, but we are not afraid to disagree when they err." Michael A. G. Haykin, *Rediscovering the Church Fathers: Who They Were and How They Shaped the Church* (Wheaton, IL: Crossway, 2011), 29.

pillars and ornaments in the church of God. Yet may they not be compared with the word of God. We may not build upon them: we may not make them the foundation and warrant of our conscience: we may not put our trust in them. Our trust is in the name of the Lord.[24]

In seeking to glean wisdom about the pastoral office from the great tradition for ministers today, we are not offering a full-fledged philosophy of ministry, a definitive view of the church fathers, or a systematic critique of modern ministry models. Rather, we seek to offer broad reflections on pastoral ministry while in conversation with patristic mentors. We write this book for pastors, churches, and students alike, with our own beloved communities in mind. We hope you are encouraged and challenged along the way. May we slow our lives, walk the parish of our local church, tend to the stillness of our soul with God, and learn from the traditions of old as we love God and neighbor. Join us as we travel ancient roads and bring back treasure to share with those we love and serve.

---

24 Barrington R. White, "Why Bother with History?" *Baptist History and Heritage* 4 (July 1969): 85 and Haykin, *Rediscovering the Church Fathers*, 29.

PART 1

THE VIRTUES AND
SPIRITUAL LIFE
OF A PASTOR

1

The Humble Pastor and
Basil of Caesarea

*Nothing is left to inflate your arrogance, O man, since
your boasting and hope now lies in mortifying yourself
in all things and seeking the life to come in Christ.*

BASIL OF CAESAREA

*Do nothing from selfish ambition or conceit, but in
humility count others more significant than yourselves.*

PHILIPPIANS 2:3

I (COLEMAN) REMEMBER HEARING all sorts of messages from
gifted preachers and teachers in my seminary chapel. To be sure,
I truly enjoyed chapel. The regular rhythm of worship, gathering
with other ministers in training, and hearing God's word was
a formative time for me. As a trumpet player, I loved that our
chaplain brought his trumpet along and blasted his horn with
the hymns. It took a couple of years, however, for me to notice

a pattern. Often, chapel preachers came from larger churches and visibly successful ministries. While there is nothing innately wrong with big churches, the subtext of these messages was "Unless you are like this kind of preacher or have this level of success in ministry, then something is wrong." No one said it, but it was hard to avoid the conclusion. Ministry success equated to influence and growth. Never once do I remember hearing a clear message on how ministry success related to a pastor's level of humility. It may have been briefly stated, but when accolades and church sizes were announced before every speaker's message, it was hard to hear anything else being said. Ambition, not self-denial, appeared to be the key to successful ministry. Unfortunately, those who buy into this lie may find themselves in a state of burnout or ministry disqualification before long. Humility, not ambition, it turns out, is the key to ministry success.[1]

We want to begin with humility in our exploration of ancient pastoral habits because this virtue is increasingly threatened in our decadent culture of virtue-signaling and social media-fueled bravado. Our disordered hearts are seeking a lesser, not greater, glory. But when we seek what is greatest through a posture of humility, we attain something that no social media influencer can provide.

Humility and Happiness

Gavin Ortlund observes that "pursuing our own glory is pathetic and boring. But seeking the glory of Jesus Christ is the most thrilling, enthralling adventure you could ever spend your life on."[2]

---

1 The chapter is an adaption of Coleman M. Ford, "'Striving for Glory with God:' Humility as the Good Life in Basil of Caesarea's Homily," *Themelios* 44, no. 2 (2019): 278–90. Used by permission.

2 Gavin Ortlund, *Humility: The Joy of Self-Forgetfulness* (Wheaton, IL: Crossway, 2023), 68.

Humility is all about rightly directed glory. Glorifying self will always lead to ruin; a humble life glorifying God always leads to happiness—true happiness.

Yet, though it brings supreme happiness, humility is not the default of our hearts. The fathers recognized this reality, noting that pride was indicative of our sinful condition and destructive to our souls. They agreed with Solomon that "one's pride will bring him low, but he who is lowly in spirit will obtain honor" (Prov. 29:23). Honor, at least the type of honor that matters in the sight of God, is obtained through a lowly spirit and humble heart. The halls of God's kingdom are decorated not with portraits of triumphant generals but of lowly servants. Each placard beneath the picture tells a tale not of a champion of human strength and ambition but of a victor crowned through humble faith and self-denial.

In his Sermon on the Mount, Jesus thoughtfully carved out this image of a humble kingdom servant. His words expressed aspirations of happiness but in a manner completely unexpected by this world. New Testament scholar Jonathan Pennington rightly translates Jesus's introductory words as "Flourishing are the ones."[3] This translation clarifies the paradoxical nature of lowliness in the kingdom of God: those who flourish best in God's kingdom arrive there by the road of humility.

In the church, pastors are the guides in the life of humility, pointing the way to Christ for all other humble pilgrims on the road to the Celestial City.[4] Augustine described the pastoral task like this:

---

3 Jonathan T. Pennington, *The Sermon on the Mount and Human Flourishing: A Theological Commentary* (Grand Rapids, MI: Baker Academic, 2017).

4 This is represented by Evangelist and other characters found in John Bunyan's famous allegory of the Christian life, *Pilgrim's Progress*.

"I feed you on what I am fed on myself. I am just a waiter, I am not the master of the house; I set food before you from the pantry which I too live on, from the Lord's storerooms."[5] Pastors thus lead others toward humility as they seek it for themselves. Knowing how much they lack, they exhort others (and themselves) to seek the gentle and lowly Savior whose heart is always for the broken and downtrodden. Dane Ortlund reminds us,

> For the penitent, his heart of gentle embrace is never outmatched by our sins and foibles and insecurities and doubts and anxieties and failures. For lowly gentleness is not one way Jesus occasionally acts toward others. Gentleness is who he is. It is his heart. He can't un-gentle himself toward his own any more than you or I can change our eye-color.[6]

At various seasons of our (Shawn's and Coleman's) own pastoral ministry, we have seen when the desire to serve others has really been a mask for extolling ourselves and our own agendas. We have been tempted to see the title "pastor" as a means toward honor and prestige in our community. We have focused too much on what others think of us and our preaching and not enough on how we are encouraging others to love and lean on Christ.

Thus, when we first read Basil's homily on humility, it cut us to the heart. Like a microscope applied to cancerous cells, Basil perceived the disease of all our souls. We discovered that the therapy we need was not self-actualization but self-denial; the cure for

---

5 Augustine, *Sermons 306–340A on the Saints*, ed. John E. Rotelle, trans. Edmund Hill, vol. 9, *The Works of Saint Augustine: A Translation for the 21st Century* (Hyde Park, NY: New City, 1994), 282.

6 Dane Ortlund, *Gentle and Lowly: The Heart of Christ for Sinners and Sufferers* (Wheaton, IL: Crossway, 2020) 21.

this cancer was an infusion of life-saving grace, which led to life-transforming humility. As physicians of the soul, pastors offer the same medicine that they themselves depend on. Let's now explore Basil's wisdom, including the ways it collides with the wisdom of this world when it comes to theories of the good life.

Basil of Caesarea

Basil of Caesarea (c. 330–379) was a significant theological force in the fourth century. On the heels of the Council of Nicaea (325), he sought to steer the church through tumultuous theological waters amid the ongoing Arian controversy and its numerous aberrant theological descendants. He was instrumental in defending the deity of the Holy Spirit and promoting a robust Trinitarianism in the spirit of Nicaea. Ordained bishop of Caesarea in 370, he remained in close relationship with various political figures and helped to establish various church leaders throughout the region of Cappadocia. These leaders—including his brother, Gregory of Nyssa, and his close friend Gregory Nazianzus—were also sympathetic to the Nicene cause.

In addition to being a significant theological voice, Basil was also a monastic reformer and minister who addressed various pastoral matters. Overall, one of his main concerns was promoting humility as integral to a flourishing Christian life and ministry.

The Chief Virtue

Basil viewed humility as the chief Christian virtue. He wrote on this topic throughout his career but his thoughts are most clearly seen in a sermon he preached around 375, now titled *On Humility*. Humility, according to Basil, was especially important for church leaders. Michael Haykin notes, "A key area in Basil's thinking about monastic and episcopal leadership was the responsibility of the monastic leader and bishop to be a man marked by humility."[7] Only through the practice of humility may one truly develop character and cultivate happiness. More importantly, humility served as the divine entrance to restoring the glory that humans lost through pride. In fact, it was in this way that humility led to happiness (because it allowed one to comprehend and fully value the life of Christ) and produced excellence of character (by allowing one to properly apply other virtues without being clouded by corrupt human pretension). The world strives for glory by means of power and personal exaltation, but this delusive pathway to glory impairs the performance of even basic virtues.

Humility in the World, Scripture, and the Christian Life

Philosopher Peter Kreeft observes that the traditional virtues of justice, wisdom, courage, and moderation are the "hinge" virtues of life, that is the virtues "on which all other virtues turn."[8] As such they are the natural virtues (described by Plato) from which the theological virtues of faith, hope, and love bloom.[9] These virtues make up "the necessary foundation and precondition for all the others."[10] Kreeft affirms that while these virtues are more fully realized by the biblical witness, they are nonetheless part of natural revelation as well.[11] In other words, they are naturally revealed and thus able to be demonstrated by all people.

---

7 Michael A. G. Haykin, *Rediscovering the Church Fathers: Who They Were and How They Shaped the Church* (Wheaton, IL: Crossway, 2009), 111.

8 Peter Kreeft, *Back to Virtue: Traditional Moral Wisdom for Modern Moral Confusion* (San Francisco: Ignatius, 1992), 68.

9 Kreeft, *Back to Virtue*, 59.

10 Kreeft, *Back to Virtue*, 59.

11 Kreeft, *Back to Virtue*, 67.

While Basil recognized the existence of natural virtues, he also affirmed the human inability to naturally practice virtue to its fullest extent. For Basil, man had "lost the good which it was in his power to possess."[12] This fall from glory came through pride, and humility was the necessary key to unlocking divine glory. In his words, "The surest salvation for him, the remedy of his ills, and the means of restoration to his original state is in practicing humility and not pretending that he may lay claim to any glory through his own efforts but seeking it from God."[13] Human effort falls short of the glory of God. Striving for glory by means of self-righteousness, worldly wisdom, and attempts at courage and moderation all fall short of their full expression in a Christian life of virtue.

To support this point, Basil provided numerous biblical examples. In a book on monastic practices, Basil stated, "Humility is to consider all (human beings) better to oneself according to the definition of the Apostle."[14] Here, Basil was referring to Paul's words in Philippians 2:3, but he was also alluding to the full apostolic testimony regarding Christ. Thus, the fundamental basis of humility for the believer is the life of Christ through the teachings of the apostles. Basil explained, "Indeed, we find that everything the Lord did is a lesson in humility"[15] and "Come, let us imitate [the apostles], so that out of our humility there may arise for us everlasting glory, the perfect and true gift of Christ."[16]

---

12 St. Basil the Great, *Homily* 20, sec. 1 in *On Christian Doctrine and Practice*, ed. John Behr and Augustine Casiday, trans. Mark DelCogliano, Popular Patristics Series 47 (Yonkers, NY: St Vladimir's Seminary Press, 2012).
13 Basil, *Homily* 20.1.
14 Anna M. Silvas, *The Asketikon of St. Basil the Great*, Oxford Early Christian Studies (Oxford: Oxford University Press, 2005), 380.
15 Basil, *Homily* 20.6.
16 Basil, *Homily* 20.6.

Imitating such humility informed all other actions in one's life, especially charity, and led to glory.[17] Christ shared his glory with those who glorified him through their actions of love. He also "allowed the temporal authorities to exercise the power given them. . . . Thus he experienced every stage of human existence from birth to death. And after such great humility, only then did he manifest his glory, giving a share of his glory to those who had glorified him."[18]

But how does one imitate Christ in this way? In his *Shorter Rules* Basil described just that. First, believers should call to mind the words and example of Christ. Next, they should claim the promise of Christ that he who humbles himself will be exalted (Luke 14:11). Last, they must remember that developing humility is akin to learning a craft, requiring practice and fraught with difficulty, though it is "accomplishing every virtue in accordance with the commandment of our Lord Jesus Christ."[19]

To provide a contrast to this, Basil also set forth the Israelites and the devil as examples of a lack of humility. Thus, the Christian grows in humility by modeling Christ and the apostles and shunning the path of Satan, which is, in essence, one of pride.

According to Mark DelCogliano, "though [Basil's] homily is entitled *On Humility*, it is as much, if not more, about pride."[20]

---

17 For more on Basil's understanding of social action and charity see Anthony Meredith, *The Cappadocians* (Crestwood, NY: St. Vladimir's Seminary Press, 1995), 27–29. See also Timothy Patitas, "St. Basil's Philanthropic Program and Modern Microlending Strategies for Economic Self-Actualization," in *Wealth and Poverty in Early Church and Society*, ed. Susan R. Holman, Holy Cross Studies in Patristic Theology and History (Grand Rapids, MI: Baker Academic, 2008), 267–86; St. Basil the Great, *On Social Justice*, trans. C. Paul Schroeder, Popular Patristics Series 38 (Crestwood, NY: St Vladimir's Seminary Press, 2009).

18 Basil, *Homily* 20.6.

19 Silvas, *Asketikon of St. Basil*, 381.

20 Mark DelCogliano, "Introduction to Homily on Humility" in *On Christian Doctrine and Practice*, St. Basil the Great, Popular Patristics Series 47 (Yonkers, NY: St. Vladimir's Seminary Press, 2012), 104.

Basil began his homily by saying that man enjoyed glory with God, which provided true nobility, wisdom, and happiness, but forfeited this by becoming prideful or "looking for something better and striving for what he could not attain."[21] This striving was giving into Satan's temptation in Genesis 3, which promised equal status with God. Instead of enjoying the good they were given, humanity fell from glory. This shows us that pride "blinds without purpose" and "causes vain haughtiness."[22] It is like an inflammation on a tumor that grows and pervades the body, becoming "a cause of death."[23] In the end, the proud will be humbled, either by choice or by consequence.

Yet, just as humanity lost the glory of God by rejecting humility, so did God bring them back to glory by entering their humanity through humility. Thus, it is not human beings who ascend to God but God who descends to them—the road to ascension begins with a posture of condescension. This is the ironic nature of the distinctly Christian virtue of humility. Basil consistently lamented that humanity spent much time posturing and seeking success in the eyes of the world but that this was a search for validation in the eyes of people and would not lead to the glory it was seeking. It prevented human beings from the true practice of virtue and thus the glory that waited at the end. "What truly exalts a person," said Basil, is "to know in truth what is great and to cling to it, and to seek the glory which comes from the Lord of Glory."[24]

In addition to calling out pride, Basil also recognized the reality of false humility. Self-exaltation can easily be disguised as humility.

21 Basil, *Homily* 20.1.
22 Basil, *Homily* 20.1.
23 Basil, *Homily* 20.1.
24 Basil, *Homily* 20.3

To support this point, Basil highlighted examples in the Bible of those who appeared to be submitting to God yet were ultimately subject to fear and arrogance. Peter, who declared his dedication to Christ, eventually denied him out of fear. This was because his avowal to stand by Christ was actually rooted in arrogance. Similarly, the Pharisee in Luke 18:11–14, though seemingly humble through total submission to God's law, "lost the righteousness in which he could boast because of his sin of pride."[25] Basil further warned that attempts at humility could easily lead to contentious behavior and "make us as bad as those fighting over the first seats," that is, James and John (Mark 10:37).[26]

According to Basil, allowing oneself to be served by another is just as much an act of humility as one performing the action itself. He declared, "The subordinate therefore need have no fear of undermining his goal of humility if he ever is ministered to by a greater."[27] Thus Basil maintained that humility can only properly flourish within a mutual relationship. Roberta Bondi helpfully explains Basil's view when she says,

> The basic attitude of humility recognizes that no person loves or does any good without the help of God, so that whatever acts of kindness or virtue a person performs, whatever strength or happiness one has, one's ability to work well and to love well— all these are possible because God gives them to the creatures as God's good gifts. No one is in a position to look down on another from a superior height because of her or his hard work or piety or mental superiority. We are all vulnerable, all limited

25 Basil, *Homily* 20.4.
26 Silvas, *Asketikon of St. Basil*, 219.
27 Silvas, *Asketikon of St. Basil*, 232.

and we each have a different struggle only God is in a position to judge.[28]

Overall, Basil affirmed that everyone needed to practice humility and receive acts wrought from a position of humility and that such mutual submission should be practiced in order to aid one another's growth in virtue by providing models for emulation and ongoing encouragement.

Lessons for Today

As we have seen, Basil continually asserted the centrality of humility in the Christian life. The implications of practicing humility are myriad for Christians, but based on this short study, we'd like to highlight three applications for pastors.

First, humility is indispensable to the Christian life and pastoral office. Modern voices have recognized the loss of teachings on Christian virtues like this one, and perhaps it is this lack that has led to a misunderstanding of holy living.[29] Virtue is not a self-driven effort fueled by innate ability, as both ancient and modern philosophers would contend, but is cultivated when one submits to the will of God. Pursuing holiness is a vital facet of the Christian life, and according to Basil, it leads to happiness in the light of Christ and his work on our behalf. Thus, humility is the axis on which Christian virtue turns.

---

28 Roberta C. Bondi, *To Love as God Loves: Conversations with the Early Church* (Philadelphia: Fortress, 1987), 43.

29 For more on virtue and Christian morality in modernity see Francis A. Schaeffer, *How Should We Then Live?: The Rise and Decline of Western Thought and Culture* (Wheaton, IL: Crossway, 2005); Alasdair MacIntyre, *After Virtue: A Study in Moral Theory*, 3rd ed. (Notre Dame: University of Notre Dame Press, 2007); David F. Wells, *Losing Our Virtue: Why the Church Must Recover Its Moral Vision* (Grand Rapids, MI: Eerdmans, 1999).

How often do pastors exhort their congregation to virtue? We contend along with Basil that pastors need to cultivate Christ-like virtue in their own lives and prompt others to follow. For example, we can humble ourselves by equipping the community of faith to practice their gifts, serve, and take ownership of ministries—even if we feel like we could do it better. Sometimes the most humble thing we can do in ministry is to let someone else do the work.

Second, humility is the proper response to receiving the gift of salvation. Commenting on Basil's theology, Haykin observes, "Foundational to humility . . . is the recognition by men and women that they are entirely destitute of all true righteousness and holiness."[30] For Basil, converting to Christ leads to humility and informs one's entire Christian life. The turn from gazing on self to gazing on God and his work of salvation on our behalf is what truly brings glory to one's life. Thus, the degree to which pastors reflect on their salvation is the degree to which they grow in humility. Calling the saints to consider the riches of Christ, not the supposed riches of a church ministry or personality, brings transformation and sustained spiritual growth. Our glory is only found in recognizing the glory of God intimately displayed in the humility of Christ. In our preaching, teaching, and discipleship, humility should be commended as the proper response to God's grace in salvation.

Third, the practice of humility serves as an apologetic to the unbeliever. Too often the world sees the story of moral failure play out in the pastorate. The desire to gain influence at the expense of humility leads to downfall. Every time. God's word predicts it

---

30 Haykin, *Rediscovering the Church Fathers*, 113.

(Prov. 16:18–19). On the other hand, a humble pastor may not draw a crowd, but he is certainly modeling Christlike behavior, and such humility has an irresistible gravitational force. It has the power to demonstrate another way of life that brings meaning and speaks hope to despair.

Happiness is the goal of every human, yet only in Christ is it achieved and properly understood. The idea of the good life, plastered on billboards and extolled in the latest pop song, is only found in a life of Christlike humility. A humble pastor whose focus is on the humble Christ will thus offer a distinct witness in a decadent culture of selfishness and pride.

Conclusion

James tells us, "God opposes the proud but gives grace to the humble" (James 4:6). Paul exhorts the church to "do nothing from selfish ambition or conceit, but in humility count others as more significant than yourselves" (Phil. 2:3). Conceit and selfish ambition are destroyers of godliness; they spread like wildfire through a church or ministry, burning and destroying souls in their path of savagery. Such pride hurts the church. But humility lifts it up to the glory of God.

In his homily, Basil taught that humility is essential for obtaining the good life. This good life is a return to the glory that humanity once had with God at the beginning of creation. Pride, the chief reason for humanity's fall from glory, continues to impair their practice of virtue. Their wisdom and ability to perform virtue are illusory. Only humility can return them to the state of glory they once possessed. Thankfully, Christ has provided a way back to glory—by humbly trusting in his salvation and imitating his humble spirit.

Because of humility's prime place in the Christian life, other virtues can only rightly be practiced through confessing weakness. Humility thus produces excellence of character and true happiness by allowing one to properly apply other virtues, free from corrupt human pretension. This applies to all aspects of life, including ministry. Therefore, pastoral virtue is found in the spirit of the humble Christ. What the world wants to gain through prideful living can only be found in humble submission to God, and pastors can present this true glory with their humble words and their humble work.

2

The Spiritual Pastor and
Gregory of Nyssa

*This truly is the vision of God: never to be satisfied in
the desire to see him. But one must always, by looking
at what he can see, rekindle his desire to see more.*

GREGORY OF NYSSA

*May the God of peace himself sanctify you completely,
and may your whole spirit and soul and body be kept
blameless at the coming of our Lord Jesus Christ.*

1 THESSALONIANS 5:23

SPIRITUALITY IS ALL ABOUT the active role of the Spirit in the
life of the Christian. More specifically, Christian spirituality refers
to God's transforming of humanity by taking them on a heavenly
journey that involves contemplating and loving him as well as cultivating ethical and virtuous practices (e.g., loving others). While
the fathers of the church conducted theology in a way that may

feel familiar to us, they addressed the spiritual matters of the soul differently than we often do. Those teaching Christian theology today may not always include spirituality, but the fathers explored spirituality from the start, thus modeling Christian reflection that balances philosophical thought with holy living.[1]

So what can the fathers teach us about spirituality? Studying textual criticism and the search for the historical Jesus ignited my (Shawn's) desire to start reading the fathers and other early Christian literature. As I dug deeper and deeper into critical theory, I felt the cold, crisp winds of spiritual apathy move over my heart. But what I found in the fathers was that they modeled how even a philologist possesses deep spiritual commitments. They showed me how creative exegesis and theological depth are for the good of the church and how Christian spirituality is the ascent of the soul toward the God we study.

According to the fathers, spirituality should be both a personal and corporate priority for the gospel minister. Though spirituality may seem mystical or subjective, it simply refers to the divine life of God, and in particular, the Spirit of God, at work in the life of the Christian. Christian spirituality thus cannot exist outside the Spirit's activities. He helps individual believers and the church contemplate God (theology), interpret Scripture (hermeneutics), and conduct their lives (ethics).[2] While spirituality can be private and invisible, it will not remain within the private realm as it also includes public activities and visible practices of virtue. Overall, in

---

1   For example, see Coleman M. Ford, "'He Who Consoles Us Should Console You': The Spirituality of the Word in Select Letters of Augustine of Hippo," *Evangelical Quarterly* 89, no. 3 (2018): 240–57.

2   This description will appear in a forthcoming chapter on patristic spirituality: Shawn J. Wilhite, "Spirituality in the Patristic Era," in *Early Christian Doctrine*, ed. Michael A. G. Haykin and Michael Strickland (Bellingham, WA: Lexham Press, forthcoming).

the classical tradition, Christian spirituality is inherently Trinitarian, displayed in the fruits of the Spirit, described as an ascent of the soul to God, and practiced in daily rhythms.

Trinitarian Spirituality

First and foremost, classical Christian spirituality is thoroughly Trinitarian. The Father, Son, and Holy Spirit have unique activities in the life of the Christian and are the source of the Christian's piety. The Son and Spirit enter the human fray, sent from the Father. Upon conversion, the Christian now houses the indwelling Spirit, is united with the Son, and is adopted and accepted by the Father. In this way, God enables humanity to be united to the divine life.

Baptism serves as a Christian's first public confession of entering into the life of the Trinity. In fact, the Matthean version of the baptismal formula has an intrinsic Trinitarian framework, concluding with "in the Name of the Father and of the Son and of the Holy Spirit" (Matt. 28:19). Scott Swain rightly says this passage provides "the basic grammar of the Bible's Trinitarian discourse."[3] The singular "Name" is matched with the three Persons to affirm one God and the three Persons identified as God.

Romans 8 also includes Trinitarian language in its discussion of the new life of a Christian. In particular, verses 12 to 17 contain themes of union with Christ, life in the Spirit, and Trinitarian activities. It reads,

> So then, brothers, we are debtors, not to the flesh, to live according to the flesh. For if you live according to the flesh you will die, but if by the Spirit you put to death the deeds of the

3 Scott R. Swain, *The Trinity: An Introduction*, Short Studies in Systematic Theology (Wheaton, IL: Crossway, 2020), 28–34.

body, you will live. For all who are led by the Spirit of God are sons of God. For you did not receive the spirit of slavery to fall back into fear, but you have received the Spirit of adoption as sons, by whom we cry, "Abba! Father!" The Spirit himself bears witness with our spirit that we are children of God, and if children, then heirs—heirs of God and fellow heirs with Christ, provided we suffer with him in order that we may also be glorified with him.

In other words, believers have received the Spirit to secure their adoption by the Father and union with the Son, and the Spirit internally confirms this adoption. Thus, the spiritual pastor is one who grounds his guidance of others in the Trinity's work on the soul, always explaining such work in a way that expresses just how the three Persons are uniquely involved in the Christian life.

Fruits of the Spirit

Externally, Trinitarian spirituality is displayed by the fruits of the Spirit as described in Galatians 5:22–25. This list of virtues show us what the active spiritual life looks like. Christians, through the work of the Spirit, display "love, joy, peace, patience, kindness, goodness, faithfulness, gentleness, self-control" and fight against "sexual immorality, impurity, sensuality, idolatry, sorcery, enmity, strife, jealousy, fits of anger, rivalries, dissensions, divisions, envy, drunkenness, orgies, and things like these."

Thus, the spiritual pastor must fill his life with the good things of the Spirit and not feed or gratify the desires of the flesh, that is, the force of sin within that battles against the Spirit.[4] Yet, while pastors

---

4 John M. G. Barclay, *Obeying the Truth: A Study of Paul's Ethics in Galatians* (Edinburgh: T&T Clark, 1988).

are called to walk in the Spirit, the Spirit is primarily the one who battles the flesh. This spiritual battle is already underway in the pastor's inner life. When he gives into temptation, he will lead people away from God. But when he displays love, joy, peace, patience, kindness, goodness, faithfulness, gentleness, and self-control, the life of God and divine qualities are communicated through him.

The Spiritual Ascent of the Soul

One way that the fathers described Christian spirituality was as the soul's ascent to God. This theme occupied the attention of several individuals, including Origen, Augustine, and Gregory of Nyssa, who defined this ascent as the Christian's journeying upward to God's presence.[5] From this perspective, a Christian's life is viewed as a movement from low to high, death to life, and earthly to heavenly.

I (Shawn) remember the first time I began to see this vision in the Scriptures. For years, I would reflect on the first half of Hebrews 12 about running the race and spiritual discipline. But I would stop short of completing the chapter, which reads,

But you have come to Mount Zion and to the city of the living God, the heavenly Jerusalem, and to innumerable angels in festal gathering, and to the assembly of the firstborn who are enrolled

---

5 For example, Augustine wrote, "What then do I love when I love my God? Who is he who is higher than the highest element in my soul? Through my soul I will ascend to him. I will rise above the force by which I am bonded to the body and fill its frame with vitality. It is not by that force that I find my God." Augustine, *Saint Augustine: Confessions*, trans. Henry Chadwick, Oxford World's Classics (Oxford: Oxford University Press, 1998). For more on the ascent of the soul in patristic theology see Don. W. Springer and Kevin M. Clarke, eds., *Patristic Spirituality: Classical Perspectives on Ascent in the Journey to God*, Studies in Theology and Religion 30 (Leiden: Brill, 2022).

in heaven, and to God, the judge of all, and to the spirits of the righteous made perfect, and to Jesus, the mediator of a new covenant, and to the sprinkled blood that speaks a better word than the blood of Abel.

Here, the journey toward true rest in Zion (Heb. 3–4) is used as a metaphor for the Christian life. On earth, Christians are in exile, walking in the desert while awaiting true Zion's arrival, and spiritual reflection on God—by the Spirit and because of the Son—is what will help them ascend to the heights of Zion.

The Beatitudes in Matthew 5 also present these earthly and heavenly dichotomies. Mourning, for example, is part of the flourishing life and leads to receiving the heavens (Matt. 5:3–4). Further, in Philippians 3:1–10, Paul reflects on his human achievement as mere rubbish compared to the surpassing worth of knowing Christ Jesus and then reflects on his spiritual progress:

Not that I have already obtained this or am already perfect, but I press on to make it my own, because Christ Jesus has made me his own. Brothers, I do not consider that I have made it my own. But one thing I do: forgetting what lies behind and straining forward to what lies ahead, I press on toward the goal for the prize of the upward call of God in Christ Jesus. (Phil. 3:12–14)

Overall, the concept of the soul's ascent is not one of detached mysticism. It is a metaphor for the spiritual birth of a Christian, the upward journey to God throughout one's life, and the completion of our human life in dwelling with God. Human life is essentially spiritual and tied to the work of the Spirit—he joins and accompanies us.

Thus, the spiritual pastor is one who not only attends to administrative tasks but also his upward wayfaring, regularly taking stock of his soul and drinking deep from the well of Christ. The pastor who does not do this is bound to produce a self-sufficient ministry, which may lead to burnout.

Developing Sacred Rhythms

I (Shawn) give thanks to God for one of my local pastors who speaks about sacred rhythms. Our corporate service includes rituals of confession, recitation, silence, and order, and our pastor also encourages us to use daily liturgies. These rituals shape and influence our spiritual commitments. Daily liturgies in particular make the mundane holy.[6]

Overall, the purpose of using these rituals is to slow one's life by rejecting needless chaos and pressure from the outside world and thus developing a keener spiritual direction. By slowing down, you can become more deeply aware of being known by God and knowing him in return. He already knows you entirely; you slow down to know him more intimately.

In *The Common Rule*, Justin Earley offers basic guidelines for personal liturgies. He suggests that on a daily basis, you could kneel three times a day in prayer, share a meal with others, spend one hour without your phone, or read Scripture before using your phone. On a weekly basis, you could talk with a friend for an hour, physically rest for a few hours, or fast from something for twenty-four hours.[7] We (Coleman and Shawn) both enjoy writing, so one morning we purposely fasted from writing. We sat outside with a

---

6   Tish Harrison Warren, *Liturgy of the Ordinary: Sacred Practices in Everyday Life* (Downers Grove, IL: InterVarsity, 2016).

7   Justin Whitmel Earley, *The Common Rule: Habits of Purpose for an Age of Distraction* (Downers Grove, IL: IVP, 2019).

cup of coffee, prayed for a few hours, and returned to our study. Surprisingly, we still wrote everything we needed to.

Thus, the spiritual pastor is one who identifies daily and weekly (even monthly or yearly) habits that reflect his values, evaluates what habits negatively and positively affect his spiritual life, and embraces the idea of slowing down. Many pastors fear slowing down. But people want to receive help from someone who has met with God. People do not need a busier minister or another activity to attend; they need a pastor who knows their name, is close with God, and can administer the medicine of Christ to them.

Gregory of Nyssa

Gregory of Nyssa (c. 335/40–395) was one such pastor. Overall, he is often regarded as the most speculative and mystical thinker of the Greek fathers.[8] Centuries after his death, the Second Council of Nicaea (787) rendered him the "father of fathers."[9] Gregory was the younger brother of Basil of Caesarea and Macrina the Younger. While Basil studied in Constantinople and Athens,[10] Gregory remained at home and received an education from Basil and Macrina. At this time, Gregory was practicing asceticism and performing ministry, but in the 360s he underwent a spiritual crisis, impelled by his adolescent rebellion, and pursued a secular career instead.[11] In

---

8   Anna M. Silvas, *Gregory of Nyssa: The Letters Introduction, Translation and Commentary*, Supplements to Vigilae Christianae 83 (Leiden: Brill, 2007), 1. This summary of Gregory's life is adapted from Shawn J. Wilhite, "Gregory of Nyssa: The Father of Fathers," *Credo Magazine* 10, no. 2 (2020). Used by permission.

9   *Acta*, sixth session, sec. 5 in *The Acts of the Second Council of Nicaea (787)*, trans. Richard Price, vol. 5 (Liverpool: Liverpool University Press).

10 Philip Rousseau, *Basil of Caesarea*, Transformation of the Classical Heritage 20 (Berkeley, CA: University of California Press, 1998), 27–60.

11 Martha Vinson, trans., *St. Gregory of Nazianzus: Select Orations*, Fathers of the Church 107 (Washington, DC: The Catholic University of America Press, 2003), 30–35.

372, Basil persuaded Gregory to return to ecclesiastical life, though he was reluctant to take the episcopate office and was filled with great self-doubt.[12] Shortly after, Gregory suffered the consecutive deaths of his wife (378),[13] Basil (379), and Macrina (379).

In 381, Gregory attended the Council of Constantinople. After this council, he was named along with ten others as those "whose teaching is to be considered normative for the interpretation of orthodoxy"[14] He was also listed as a standard bearer of Nicene orthodoxy by Theodosius.[15]

In Gregory's final years, he became increasingly focused on holy living. He wrote various works of spirituality at the time, including *The Life of Moses* (c. 392) and *Homilies on the Song of Songs*. Both books focus on the inner life of the Christian who is drawn upward to God. Jean Daniélou describes Gregory's theology of ascent as moving from light to darkness, embracing knowledge and mystery, and participating in God. In Daniélou's words, Gregory taught that God

is truly known insofar as the soul participates in Him. To know God "in the mirror of the soul" and to know Him in the

---

12 Sister Agnes Clare Way, trans., *Saint Basil: Letters, Volume 2 (186–368)*, Fathers of the Church 28 (Washington, DC: The Catholic University of America Press, 1955), 139–40.

13 Gregory most likely married in his youth and then became celibate after his wife's death. See Bradley K. Storin, trans., *Gregory of Nazianzus's Letter Collection: The Complete Translation* (Oakland, CA: University of California Press, 2019), 102–3. Andrew Louth, "The Cappadocians," in *The Cambridge History of Early Christian Literature*, ed. Frances Young, Lewis Ayres, and Andrew Louth (Cambridge: Cambridge University Press, 2004), 297–98.

14 Khaled Anatolios, *Retrieving Nicaea: The Development and Meaning of Trinitarian Doctrine* (Grand Rapids, MI: Baker Academic, 2011), 158.

15 Sozomen, *History of the Church* 7.9.6, in *Nicene and Post-Nicene Fathers, Second Series*, trans. Chester D. Hartranft (Peabody, MA: Hendrickson, 1994), 2:381. *Codex Theodosianus* 16.1.3 in *The Theodosian Code and Novels and the Sirmondian Constitutions*, trans. Clyde Pharr (Princeton, NJ: Princeton University Press, 1952).

Darkness are not two different experiences, but two aspects of the same phenomenon. . . . Mystical knowledge is thus always a mixture of knowledge and ignorance, possession and quiet, immanence and Transcendence—it is a "luminous Darkness." This imperfect awareness is the only authentic knowledge of God, inasmuch as it retrains within the finite area of knowledge the infinite realm of ignorance.[16]

The Ascent of Moses and the Christian

Gregory came to these beliefs through his study of Scripture, and his exegesis models one way to read the Bible for spiritual formation. In *The Life of Moses*, Gregory provided two kinds of readings: literary and spiritual.[17] His literary reading traced Moses's life, and his spiritual or mystical reading highlighted virtue. In his spiritual reading, he mapped the ascent of Moses from the light to darkness, physical to spiritual, and lower to higher. Commenting on Gregory's text, Frances Young explains,

> Like the nature of the infinite God, perfection is boundless, and there is no stopping place or final attainment. Human perfection is always growth in goodness. Moses' life provides a pattern: through contemplation of it we can reach some understanding of what the perfect life might be like, by treating it as a kind of map or guide to the spiritual journey.[18]

16 Jean Daniélou, "Introduction," in *From Glory to Glory: Texts from Gregory of Nyssa's Mystical Writings*, ed. Herbert Musurillo S. J. (Crestwood, NY: St. Vladimir's Seminary Press, 2001), 56.

17 Gregory of Nyssa, *Gregory of Nyssa: The Life of Moses*, trans. Abraham J. Malherbe and Everett Ferguson, The Classics of Western Spirituality (New York: Paulist, 1978).

18 Frances M. Young, *Brokenness and Blessing: Towards a Biblical Spirituality* (Grand Rapids, MI: Baker Academic, 2007), 24.

Modern readers may be tempted to think that this kind of spiritual reading of Scripture is not grounded in proper exegesis. However, the fathers' spiritual readings relied on intensive study of the Scriptures.[19] Thus, regarding his work on Moses, Gregory said, "We shall seek out the spiritual understanding which corresponds to the history in order to obtain suggestions of virtue."[20] He continued,

It is not difficult to harmonize the sequence of the history with spiritual contemplation. He who left the Egyptian behind dead in the water, was sweetened by the wood, was delighted in the apostolic springs, and was refreshed by the shade of the palm trees, is already capable of receiving God. For the rock, as the Apostle says, is Christ, who is moistureless and resistant to unbelievers, but if one should employ the rod of faith he becomes drink to those who are thirsty and flows into those who receive him.[21]

Overall, Gregory's spiritual reading of Moses strikingly combined contemplation and social engagement. First, he highlighted the

---

19 For introductory and advanced resources on patristic exegesis, see John J. O'Keefe and Russel R. Reno, *Sanctified Vision: An Introduction to Early Christian Interpretation of the Bible* (Baltimore: John Hopkins University Press, 2005); Paul M. Blowers and Peter W. Martens, eds., *The Oxford Handbook of Early Christian Biblical Interpretation* (Oxford: Oxford University Press, 2019); Paul M. Blowers, "Patristic Interpretation," in *The Oxford Encyclopedia of Biblical Interpretation*, ed. Steven L. McKenzie, vol. 2 (New York: Oxford University Press, 2013), 81–89; Michael Cameron, *Christ Meets Me Everywhere: Augustine's Early Figurative Exegesis*, Oxford Studies in Historical Theology (Oxford: Oxford University Press, 2012); Charles Kannengiesser, ed., *Handbook of Patristic Exegesis*, 2 vols., The Bible in Ancient Christianity 2 (Atlanta, GA: SBL Press, 2006); Shawn J. Wilhite, "Cyril of Alexandria's Trinitarian Exegesis" (PhD thesis, Durham University, 2022).

20 Gregory of Nyssa, *Life of Moses*, bk. 1, sec. 15.

21 Gregory, *Life of Moses* 2.136.

solitary activities of Moses and the virtues of the reader. Moses, in Midian, "lived alone in the mountains away from the turmoil of the marketplace."[22] Thus, Moses was an exemplar of the contemplative life. Gregory explained, "In the same way we shall live a solitary life, no longer entangled with adversaries or mediating between them, but we shall live among those of like disposition and mind who are fed by us while all the movements of our soul are shepherded, like sheep, by the guiding reason."[23] Yet, after spending time alone and contemplating the mysteries of God, Moses returns once more to the people in order to "share with them the marvels which had been shown to him in the theophany."[24]

In the prologue of *The Life of Moses*, Gregory explained that he used Moses as a model for the Christian contemplative life because it urges believers to move toward the heavenly ascent of God. He exhorted, "While you are competing admirably in the divine race along the course of virtue, light footedly leaping and straining constantly for the prize of the heavenly calling, I exhort, urge and encourage you vigorously to increase your speed."[25] The Christian must continue in pursuit of virtue because ceasing the pursuit of virtue begins a life of evil, which leads to death, while virtue leads to the divine life found in God.

Moses's ascent up the mountain to meet God is just like the ascent of the Christian's soul to meet with the deep mysteries of God. To contemplate God is to ascend the heights of the mountain where God dwells and consider the mysteries of God. According to Gregory,

22 Gregory, *Life of Moses* 1.19.
23 Gregory, *Life of Moses* 2.18.
24 Gregory, *Life of Moses* 1.56.
25 Gregory, *Life of Moses* 1.1.

This means that the one person who would approach the contemplation of Being must be pure in all things so as to be pure in soul and body, washed stainless of every spot in both parts, in order that he might appear pure to the One who sees what is hidden and that visible respectability might correspond to the inward condition of the soul.[26]

While Moses did not physically see God and neither do believers, Gregory asserted that contemplation of God remains unaffected by sight or hearing and is rather "customary perceptions of the mind."[27] He wrote,

The knowledge of God is a mountain steep indeed and difficult to climb—the majority of people scarcely reach its base. If one were a Moses, he would ascend higher and hear the sound of trumpets which, as the text of the history says, becomes louder as one advances. For the preaching of the divine nature is truly a trumpet blast, which strikes the hearing, being already loud at the beginning but becoming yet louder at the end.[28]

In other words, it is through preaching the eternal, divine realities of God that this spiritual life is reached. People respond to the preaching of God's word and are inspired to ascend the hill in order to contemplate the mysteries of God.

Gregory continued, saying that as Moses ascended the mountain, he passed into a dark cloud. Here, in the dark, one experiences the mysteries of God:

26 Gregory, *Life of Moses* 2.154.
27 Gregory, *Life of Moses* 2.157.
28 Gregory, *Life of Moses* 2.158.

Leaving behind everything that is observed, not only what sense comprehends but also what the intelligence thinks it sees, it keeps on penetrating deeper until by the intelligence's yearning for understanding it gains access to the invisible and the incomprehensible, and there it sees God.[29]

As believers contemplate God, they ascend the difficult mountain—not traversed by all—and consider God in the darkness. There, they rise higher and higher as the trumpets become louder and louder. God shines forth in creation, and the heavens proclaim his glory.[30]

Ascending to Perfection through Beauty

Overall, Gregory described the spiritual life as a progress of perfection.[31] While perfection is not attainable for humanity and reserved only for God, the pursuit of perfection as the pursuit of the divine life and a change from "glory to glory" is (2 Cor. 3:18). The final paragraph of Gregory's *On Perfection* points out how moving toward perfection is participating in God's life.[32] Here, he says that to be

---

29 Gregory, *Life of Moses* 2.163.

30 Gregory, *Life of Moses* 2.167–68.

31 By envisioning the spiritual ascent of the Christian as a progression toward intimacy with God, Gregory made a striking break from Platonism. Daniélou explains that while Platonists argued that mutability was evil, Gregory argued that change is brought about by God, who is the true source of goodness and virtue. Daniélou, "Introduction," 46–47. Daniélou points out this passage from Gregory's *Great Catechetical Discourse* (pt. 3, sec. 21.1): "Man (i.e., humanity) was fashioned as a copy of the divine nature . . . but by necessity being of a changeable nature; for it was not possible for him who had the beginning of [his] being from alteration not to be changeable at all; for the passage from nonbeing into existence is a sort of alteration, nonexistence being changing into being by divine power."

32 "This, therefore, is perfection in the Christian life in my judgment, namely, the participation of one's soul and speech and activities in all of the names by which Christ is signified, so that the perfect holiness, according to the eulogy of Paul, is taken upon oneself in "the whole body and soul and spirit" (1 Thess. 5:23) continuously safeguarded against being mixed with evil. . . . For does man make a change only towards evil? Indeed, it would not be possible

changed from glory to glory is the endless pursuit of participating in the divine life, namely Christ, so that one's whole self becomes more like him. Through the immutable Son, Christians can strive for perfection and progressively conform more and more to the image of the Son. Perfection, though unattainable in its fullest extent, does partially exist this side of heaven as perpetual growth toward the divine life.

Gregory then argued that the concept of beauty is what draws the soul away from evil (i.e., the privation of good) and toward the divine life.[33] Without such goading from God himself, a person cannot move toward the divine nature. Gregory explained,

> Since, therefore, every nature tends to attract what is proper to it, and the human is in some way proper to God, because

---

for him to be on the side of the good if he were by nature inclined only to a single one of the opposites. In fact, the fairest product of change is the increase of goods, the change to the better always changing what is nobly changed into something more divine. Therefore, I do not think it is a fearful thing (I mean that our nature is changeable). The Logos shows that it would be a disadvantage for us not to be able to make a change for the better, as a kind of wing of flight to greater things. Therefore, let no one be grieved if sees in his nature a penchant for change. Changing in everything for the better, let him exchange 'glory for glory' (2 Cor 3:18), becoming greater through dialing increase, ever perfecting himself, and never arriving too quickly at the limit of perfection. For this is truly perfection: never to stop growing towards what is better and never placing any limit on perfection." Gregory of Nyssa, *St. Gregory: Ascetical Works*, ed. Virginia Woods Callahan, Fathers of the Church 58 (Washington, DC: Catholic University of America Press, 1967), 122.

33 "But because our nature is impoverished of the beautiful, it always reaches toward that which it needs. This appetite for what is lacking is the desiring condition of our nature, which is either foiled of the truly beautiful through misjudgment or perhaps even obtains by chance that which is good to obtain. But the Nature which exceeds every good conception and surpasses every power, because It needs none of those things which are thought of as good, being Itself the fullness of good things, and because It is not in beauty by participation of some beauty, but is Itself the nature of the beautiful (whatever the mind may assume the beautiful to be), does not even admit the impulse of hope in Itself, for hope operates only in respect to what is not present." St. Gregory of Nyssa, *On the Soul and the Resurrection*, trans. Catharine P. Roth, Popular Patristics Series 12 (Crestwood, NY: St. Vladimir's Seminary Press, 1993), 78.

it bears in itself the imitation of its Archetype, necessarily the soul is attracted to the Divine which is related to it (for what is proper to God must come safely to Him). But if the soul is light and simple with no bodily weight holding it down, its progress towards the One who attracts it becomes pleasant and easy.[34]

In other words, because humans find their source in God and have the Son as the archetype, they are drawn to the beauty of God. Yet, it is God who woos them, sometimes using painful conditions to bring about change.[35]

Thus, this upward movement of the soul through beauty and toward perfection and union with God includes darkness. Darkness, for Gregory, is not always evil. Rather, it is God's dwelling because it is both unknown and unseen.[36] As we saw earlier, Moses's life and ascent of Mount Sinai prompted Gregory to associate darkness with the spiritual life. Just as Moses ascended the mountain to meet God in the darkness, so does the Christian ascend the mountain to meet God in the darkness.

Overall, to encounter the divine being is to experience life to the fullest.[37] Gregory summarized,

This truly is the vision of God: never to be satisfied in the desire to see him. But one must always, by looking at what he can see, rekindle his desire to see more. Thus, no limit would interrupt

---

34 Gregory, *Soul and Resurrection*, 7.

35 Gregory, *Soul and Resurrection*, 7.

36 Gregory, *Life of Moses* 2.162–69.

37 "The Divine is by its nature life-giving. Yet the characteristic of the divine nature is to transcend all characteristics. . . . True Being is true life. This Being is inaccessible to knowledge. If then the life-giving nature transcends knowledge, that which is perceived certainly is not life." Gregory, *Life of Moses*, 2.234–35.

growth in the ascent to God, since no limit to the Good can be found nor is the increasing of the desire for the Good brought to an end because it is satisfied.[38]

In sum, a spiritual ascent may lead to darkness, it will consist of mystery, and it draws upon divine beauty to satisfy the whole human person.

Conclusion

As the spiritual life of the pastor goes, so goes the spiritual life of the congregation. While it may be the case that a pastor's attention to spirituality does not affect the congregation as much as he would like, we believe the general rule holds true. Viewing our spiritual journeys as the ascent of the soul gives us a way to approach our daily lives in the study, the counseling session, and the pulpit. By the power of the Spirit, we are being drawn up further into the life of God as we meditate on God's word. And as leaders in ministry, we must model this life and call others so that they join us in the ascent and we can collectively seek purification and holiness. What we do in the daily work of ministry has deep spiritual significance, and we are called to live in the life of the triune God—bearing fruit and structuring our lifestyles around his existence—as we call others to do the same.

---

38 Gregory, *Life of Moses* 2.239.

3

The Sacramental Pastor
and Ambrose of Milan

Open, then, your ears, inhale the good savor
of eternal life which has been breathed upon
you by the grace of the sacraments.

<small>AMBROSE OF MILAN</small>

When the goodness and loving kindness of God our Savior
appeared, he saved us, not because of works done by us
in righteousness, but according to his own mercy, by the
washing of regeneration and renewal of the Holy Spirit.

<small>TITUS 3:4–5</small>

A POEM ONCE ADORNED the walls of the fourth-century baptistery constructed at the Basilica of Sant'Ambrogio in Milan, Italy. Its author was undoubtedly the bishop of Milan—Ambrose. This poem captured Ambrose's baptismal vision and was visible to all who entered the waters. It reads,

This eight-niched temple has risen to a holy purpose,
And eight sides of the font perform their task.
That number befits a chamber for baptizing,
It towers so that people may be saved.
In the splendor of Christ's rising, to break the bars
Of death and bring life out of tombs.
Freeing from sin's stain repenting men,
Cleansed in the font's pure-running stream.
Here those shedding vile crimes of their past
May wash their hearts and take away pure breasts.
Here let them swiftly come. Here anyone who dares,
However darkened, will go off whiter than snow.
Let saints run here, since no one can be saintly
Without these waters, by God's reign and plan.
Here flares the right. What can be more God's work
Than removing sin in an eyeblink?[1]

As Ambrose prepared men and women for baptism, he told them they would be immersed in the water and thus clothed with Christ. The baptistery at Milan was constructed so as to feed water from four sides, signifying the four rivers of Eden described in Genesis 2:11–14, and to provide running water in the pool through one drain, symbolizing the "living water" of eternal life that Jesus spoke of in John 4:14.[2] Ambrose wanted every detail of his basilica to convey the rich spiritual symbolism of the Christian life, a symbolism that arose out of a close reading of Scripture and a focus on

---

1   Garry Wills, *Font of Life: Ambrose, Augustine, and the Mystery of Baptism* (New York: Oxford University Press, 2012), 11.

2   For a more detailed description of Ambrose's baptistry, including the poem inscribed on the walls, see Wills, *Font of Life*, 2–13.

the otherworldly nature of the Christian faith. Thus, Ambrose is a prime example of what we'd like to call a sacramental pastor—he understood the rich spiritual realities present in the church, the preaching of Scripture, and the practices of worship. He understood the power of God conveyed through the word of God. Whether in baptism or in singing hymns, Ambrose knew God was at work through the ordinary things of the Christian faith. Before learning from his ministry, let's define what these sacraments are and show how they can affect our experience in the church.

Baptism and the Supper

In the corporate acts of baptism and the Lord's Supper, we celebrate the power of the Spirit working in the body of Christ. The Spirit is at work in all aspects of worship and ministry, but the two sacraments (or ordinances) provide special physical pictures of his powerful work of spiritual transformation. Further, the sacraments are derived from God himself and undergirded by his word. As with all the means of grace, the word and Spirit are what make the sacraments effective for spiritual growth.

In short, baptism shows the reality that saints are reborn by faith in Christ; they shed their old self and put on the new self, which is Christ. This happens as the Spirit changes their heart to love Christ, and thus baptism also shows us who is in communion and who is not. The Lord's Supper, a covenantal symbol, brings the church together to proclaim the gospel and continually grow in the Spirit as they worship him together. They are saints because they now dwell by faith in the body of Christ and will one day dwell with him for eternity (Rev 21:3).

In the church I (Coleman) grew up in, we took baptism and the Lord's Supper seriously. The Supper was a weekly celebration, and baptism was considered a requirement for salvation. This church was part of a tradition that eventually took shape following the early-nineteenth-century Cane Ridge revivals in Cane Ridge, Kentucky, what has come to be known as the Stone-Campbell (or Restoration) Movement. This movement saw the New Testament as the authority for church practice and jettisoned (or at least neglected) the historic creeds and confessions in favor of a plain and simple reading of the Bible. The spirit of the movement—reform and biblical simplicity—were worthy goals. What developed, however, was an ultra-literalistic interpretation of many New Testament passages on worship and practice. This group lacked both a broad, biblical theology of worship as well a charitable view of church history. As far as I could tell, the church of my youth did not deny core doctrines of the faith, but they certainly left them murky and unexplained. And the strict New Testament–only interpretation of the Christian life eventually led to beliefs that, in my experience, promoted a condescending perspective of other church traditions and even a pugnacious attitude toward other professing Christians. While this church also shaped me in healthy ways, I recognize that part of what was missing in my experience was a healthy view of the sacraments.

The idea of sacrament, understood in a biblically faithful and theologically correct manner, leads to more faithful Christian discipleship and more serious pastoral practice. The notion of sacrament is not foreign to Protestant worship, even Baptist worship, and has been used comfortably by past believers to highlight the biblical means of grace within the life of the church.[3] Further,

---

3   Michael Haykin has demonstrated how English Baptists inherited their understanding of the sacraments from earlier Puritan theology, which comfortably situated the sacraments of the Lord's Supper and baptism within a proper biblical framework apart from Roman Catholic sacramentalism. See Michael A. G. Haykin, *Amidst Our Beloved Saints: Recovering Sacrament in the Baptist Tradition* (Bellingham, WA: Lexham Press, 2022). For Baptist perspectives on

a sacramental understanding of our life in the church reminds us of our eschatological destiny. We are a company of saints, aided by and growing in the Spirit, on a journey toward heaven. Simon Chan explains,

> We cannot conceive of the church as a sacramental community without at the same time conceiving of it as an eschatological community. . . . Thus the signs of a sacramental community are also the signs of an eschatological community: a community on the move, whose life and mission are always directed toward the future, the *visio Dei*. This gives an eschatological seriousness to everything the church does.[4]

The notion of sacrament communicates that something other-worldly and future-bound is taking place when the saints gather for worship. It's not magic, and it's not secretive—rather, it's spiritual and transformative.

Let's look at the Supper as an example. Paul communicates something of this when he talks about participation in the body and blood of Christ. "The cup of blessing that we bless," says Paul, "is it not a participation in the blood of Christ? The bread that we break, is it not a participation in the body of Christ?" (1 Cor. 10:16). Stephen Um comments,

> The objective reality of Christ's work is subjectively appropriated by the work of the Spirit. Christ is really spiritually (but

---

the nature of the church and sacraments see Anthony R. Cross and Philip E. Thompson, eds. *Baptist Sacramentalism: Studies in Baptist History and Thought* (Eugene, OR: Pickwick, 2007).

4   Simon Chan, *Spiritual Theology: A Systematic Study of the Christian Life* (Downers Grove, IL: IVP Academic, 1998), 112.

not physically) present—but not in a mechanistic sense. The Christian's subjective experience is important—but not in an instrumental sense. In the Lord's Supper, Christians commune with God in Christ through the Holy Spirit.[5]

In other words, the meal of the Lord connects us with the body of the Lord. This is not a re-sacrifice or a transmutation of the bread and wine into the body and blood of Christ. It is a recognition of the amazing mystery that the church is bound up in the life of God in Christ. Um observes,

> The breaking of his literal body binds Christians together in his mystical body. Communion together is based on his relentless grace. . . . The Lord's supper reveals the vertical aspects of what it means to be in union with God through the Lord Jesus Christ, but there are also horizontal and social implications for what it means to put others' needs first.[6]

The Supper reminds us of the spiritual connection Christians have with the Lord and with one another. It is anything but casual as it signifies a covenantal bond (Luke 22:20; 1 Cor. 11:25). Yet, the Supper is not a conditional or contractual act; it is an act of love and gratitude for the Savior who took on flesh for our salvation. It is a gift, not a burden, to God's people. We recommit ourselves to God and one another with each sip of the cup and every bite of the bread. The Supper is a salve for the soul. Without regular participation in the Lord's Supper, a Christian will not appreciate

5   Stephen T. Um, *1 Corinthians: The Word of the Cross*, Preaching the Word (Wheaton, IL: Crossway, 2015), 205.
6   Um, *1 Corinthians*, 208–9.

the richness of God's grace given in the person and work of Christ. The sacraments also connect believers to the universal church, reminding them that every person in the body of Christ—both past and present—has participated in the living acts of baptism and the Lord's Supper. After being welcomed into the body of Christ through the baptismal waters, Christians are sustained and nourished by the life of Christ through the Supper of Christ.

Overall, ministers of the gospel handle deep and spiritual things week in and week out. Empowered by the word of God, pastors encourage the saints not with worldly things but with the mysteries and power of God. These are clearly expounded in the ministry of Ambrose, who challenges us to consider the otherworldly nature of what pastors lead the church into on a weekly basis. He not only preached on the sacraments but also encouraged other ministers to cultivate spiritual habits and led laypeople to sing songs confessing the deep mystery of God in Christ. The man behind the words of sacramental beauty carved on the walls of Milan's basilica was actually a reluctant candidate for leading the church, yet he soon became a respected (perhaps even feared) pastor and theologian. He would come to champion the sacraments of the church, and his pastoral sense led him to creatively address one of the greatest theological crises of his day.

Ambrose of Milan

In 374, the Homoian bishop of Milan named Auxentius died and left the office open. Milan became divided into Nicene and Arian factions,[7] which was as much of a civil matter as it was an

---

7 Homoians were those who confessed that the Son was of like substance with the Father, a theological middle ground between what was declared at the Council of Nicaea in 325—that the Son was of the "same substance" (*homoousios*) as the Father—and those who confessed

ecclesiastical one. As governor of the province, Ambrose (339–397) chose to intervene. Historian Neil McLynn sees this interruption as Ambrose's attempt to mediate the two positions and allow the Nicene voice to be heard amid the majority Arian party.[8] Whatever the motivation, the outcome produced something quite unexpected. Ambrose not only became the civic mediator in this situation but also the next bishop, one who would eventually bring the church into alignment with Nicene orthodoxy.[9]

Yet, Ambrose considered himself a "reluctant bishop," or, at least, a surprised bishop.[10] His election to the pastorate was neither planned nor deliberate. In fact, he actually sought to escape this pastoral call. Paulinus's biography tells us that since

> the people were about to revolt in seeking a bishop, Ambrose had the task of putting down the revolt. So he went to the church. And when he was addressing the people, the voice of a child among the people is said to have called out suddenly: "Ambrose bishop." At the sound of this voice, the mouths of all the people joined in the cry: "Ambrose bishop." Thus, those who a while before were disagreeing most violently . . . suddenly agreed on this one with miraculous and unbelievable harmony.[11]

---

that he was of a "different substance" (*anomoeans*). That said, the term "Homoian" was flexible and complex. For more on the Homoian party see Lewis Ayres, *Nicaea and Its Legacy: An Approach to Fourth-Century Trinitarian Theology* (Oxford: Oxford University Press, 2006), 133–40.

8 Neil B. McLynn, *Ambrose of Milan: Church and Court in a Christian Capital*, The Transformation of Classical Heritage 22 (Berkeley, CA: University of California Press, 1994), 43.

9 See Ayres, *Nicaea and Its Legacy*, 261.

10 McLynn, *Ambrose of Milan*, 1.

11 Paulinus of Milan, *Life of St. Ambrose*, in *The Life of Saint Ambrose: A Translation of Vita Ambrosii*, trans. Sr. Mary Simplicia Kaniecka (Washington, DC: Catholic University of America Press, 1928), 6.

Paulinus goes on to describe various actions that Ambrose immediately took in an attempt to disqualify himself and thus avoid his election. After ordering tortures to be inflicted on prisoners (though he probably did not intend to enforce these), he then pondered being a philosopher and finally tried to flee the city at midnight on the evening before the election.[12] His escape, according to Paulinus, was prevented as a matter of divine will, for God was "preparing a strong support for His Catholic church against His enemies."[13]

After failing to escape this pastoral call, Ambrose requested to be baptized by a Nicene bishop. It is unclear if this is proof that Ambrose rejected Arianism at this point in time, but it does match his later opposition to Arianism as seen early in his episcopal career at the Council of Aquileia in 381.[14] Immediately following his baptism, Ambrose quickly progressed through the lower offices of the church and was consecrated as bishop on the eighth day.[15]

As bishop (374–397), Ambrose had significant influence over not only his own flock but local leaders and Roman emperors as well.[16] Yet, he understood his primary role to be one of a shepherd, preacher, and steward of God's mysteries. Even with the ensuing Arian controversy in the foreground, Ambrose remained undaunted in the theological formation of his people. He set on a course of

---

12 Paulinus, *Life of St. Ambrose*, 7–8.

13 Paulinus, *Life of St. Ambrose*, 8.

14 For more on this episode see Daniel H. Williams, *Ambrose of Milan and the End of the Arian-Nicene Conflicts*, Oxford Early Christian Studies (Oxford: Oxford University Press, 1995), 154–84. 154–84.

15 Paulinus, *Life of St. Ambrose*, 9. These offices included deacon and priest. It was not uncommon for a special individual to go straight to bishop, thus bypassing the other traditional offices. Augustine became a bishop in this way when he entered the church at Hippo Regius. It appears that Cyprian had a similar experience in Carthage.

16 For more on Ambrose's fascinating encounter with Emperor Theodosius see Boniface Ramsey, *Ambrose*, Early Church Fathers (London: Routledge, 1997), 32.

preaching and teaching in Milan, maintaining fidelity to Nicene theology and highlighting the profound mystery represented in the acts of Christian worship practiced in the church.

The Spiritual Meaning of Physical Acts

Something special happens when the saints gather for worship. If we believe what the Scriptures say, then we should believe that God is at work when the word is preached, sung, and proclaimed in baptism and the Lord's Supper. Theologians have attempted to explain what happens spiritually when the church gathers by coining the term "sacrament," which arose early in the church's life and vocabulary to denote those elements of worship that stood apart from others, namely baptism and the Lord's Supper. These were viewed as bonds or oaths that confirmed and continually affirmed one's faith in Christ.[17] The term then developed over the centuries to become a "sacred sign . . . directly connected to the action of grace."[18]

Some church traditions believe that God's grace is imparted to Christians through various acts—like marriage and final rites—administered by the ordained priest, who has unique authority. Does this mean that the idea of sacrament is off-limits to Protestant evangelicals? Not necessarily. The Protestant Reformers argued from Scripture that the sacraments did not infuse grace in believers. This did not mean, however, that the mysterious nature of the sacraments was abolished completely: it was restored to its rightful place in light of the gospel.[19]

17 Antonio Grappone, "Sacrament (Sacramentum)," ed. Angelo Di Berardino and James Hoover, trans. Joseph T. Papa, Erik A. Koenke, and Eric E. Hewett, *Encyclopedia of Ancient Christianity*, vol. 3 (Downers Grove, IL: IVP Academic; InterVarsity Press, 2014), 449.

18 Grappone, "Sacrament (Sacramentum)," 449.

19 For a helpful summary of the Reformers on the sacraments see Bobby Jamieson, "The Reformation's Restoration of the Sacraments" 9Marks, September 26, 2017, https://www.9marks.org/.

Ambrose demonstrates that the work of the Spirit is on display in the work of the church, and when we participate in this, we witness the mystery of God at work, which is essential to the Christian life. As noted earlier, Ambrose imprinted the spiritual significance of baptism on the very walls of his church. It was a constant reminder to congregants of the freedom from sin that was signified by their baptism. This was how they entered their new life, through the "font's pure-running stream."[20] Historian Gary Wills provides a helpful overview of Ambrose's perspective of baptism:

> Ambrose had a mystical, poetic, and all-inclusive theology of Christian initiation. He saw baptism as the culmination of the entire sacred history leading up to Jesus's fulfillment of all the prophecies that pointed directly to baptism. The whole meaning of the Trinity was enacted and revealed in the action at the font, which brought new Christians into the inner dialogue of the persons with each other in the Godhead. The reality of the church was embodied in the rebirth of humanity out of the saving waters.[21]

Though baptism was a onetime act, it became an object of ongoing spiritual reflection. It also ushered Christians to the table of the Lord's Supper where they could finally partake and grow in their understanding of the significance of Christ's body and blood shed on their behalf. To help his people understand what happens at the font of baptism and the table of Christ, Ambrose wrote two texts titled *On the Mysteries* and *On the Sacraments*. While both unpack the sacraments and provide a sacramental vision for the Christian

20 Wills, *Font of Life*, 11.
21 Wills, *Font of Life*, 137.

life, *On the Mysteries* is more comprehensive and thus will serve as the focus of our discussion.

In this work, Ambrose advocated for a rich and profound vision for the Christian acts of baptism and the Lord's Supper. The term "mysteries" is a synonym for "sacraments" and is often used in place of this term in the Eastern Orthodox Church today. Ambrose was emphatic that he would only offer such teaching to the baptized (or initiated), otherwise he would be betraying these mysteries. When we learn that these words were given to newly baptized Christians during the week of Easter, we can see that this was a bold message. During the first three centuries, the church prepared candidates for baptism with instruction in faith and withheld participation in the Eucharist until their baptism rites were complete. Ambrose did the same in the church of Milan. After baptism and confirmation, the Eucharist would be taken, and the full explanation of the Christian rites would be given to those who had now been illumined by the Holy Spirit through their baptism.

In his instruction, Ambrose called his hearers to imagine the scene of their recent baptism, leading them to recall the various ministers present at the service and, more importantly, to reflect on the "grace of their ministrations."[22] Hearers entered back into the experience of their baptism to begin retracing not the physical steps of the event but the spiritual realities that took place underneath. Referencing Romans 1:20, Ambrose affirmed that the invisible things of God were understood by the visible things of creation. These baptized believers had renounced Satan and the

22 Ambrose, *De Mysteriis*, bk. 2, sec. 6, in *Saint Ambrose, Theological and Dogmatic Treatises*, trans. Roy J. Deferrari, Fathers of the Church 44 (Washington, DC: The Catholic University of America Press, 1963).

"the world with its luxury and pleasures" and entered into new life in Christ, thus embarking on a commitment to discipleship.[23] They were physically cleansed by water, but they were spiritually cleansed by the Spirit.

Biblical images of water flooded the imagination of Ambrose and he used them to saturate his hearers with a deeper understanding of God's grace floating under the surface. The idea of the Spirit's presence in the water harks back to Genesis 1 when "the Spirit of God was hovering over the face of the waters" (Gen. 1:2). The Spirit was also seen in the flood as the dove sent by Noah, carrying the wood of Christ's cross. Even the raven sent by Noah had a deeper meaning for Ambrose, representing the despair of sin. Further, Ambrose highlighted the story of bitter water at Marah during Israel's desert wandering. Only when Moses struck the water with wood did it become sweet, and the same is true of teaching baptism without the cross of Christ. The act of baptism without "the preaching of the cross of the Lord is to no advantage," and only when the message includes the cross does the "water become sweet for grace."[24]

We must try to understand Ambrose at this point. The pastor of Milan, face to face with newly minted disciples of Christ, sought to extract every ounce of spiritual meaning from the biblical text in order to instill in his hearers the marvelous depths of their new spiritual life. For Ambrose, these Old Testament images prefigured the truth of the Spirit made clear in the New Testament. Overall, Ambrose emphasized the mysterious nature of what his people experienced physically. He believed that the physical acts of the worshiping church always relayed spiritual realities.

23 Ambrose, *De Mysteriis*, chap. 2, sec. 5.
24 Ambrose, *De Mysteriis* 3.14.

As pastors, we should take seriously the connection of our baptism to the new life we have in Christ. According to Ambrose, "all disgrace is buried" and "carnal sin" is washed away.[25] Baptism is a declaration that there is a new life dedicated to Christ, one that recognizes the miracle of salvation, Christ's atonement for sin, and the Spirit's empowerment to walk in freedom from sin. Baptism represents a new divine reality in the life of the Christian as marked by the triune name of God and directed to walk in newness of life. Baptism is the recognition that both the cross of Christ and the Spirit of Christ are necessary for new life. Ambrose remarked, "For that sacrament which you receive is made what it is by the word of Christ."[26]

Just as Ambrose did in the fourth century, pastors today serve as hosts in the spiritual banquet hall of God's word. Ministry leaders guide their people through the halls of the unseen realm using the means of grace. Whether in the act of baptism, the Lord's Supper, or the preaching of God's word, shepherds in the church usher the people of God into the presence of God. While we may not always call these acts sacramental, they nonetheless provide a window into the mysterious work and eternal nature of God. To reduce such acts to anything less walks dangerously close to pagan religion—practicing rituals for ritual's sake and trying to coax a deity into action.

The Virtues of a Sacramental Pastor

According to Ambrose, pastors were stewards of God's mysteries and must acknowledge the weighty work of advocating for and applying the grace of God to the people of God. To help pastors

25 Ambrose, *De Mysteriis* 3.11.
26 Ambrose, *De Mysteriis* 9.52.

further understand this work, Ambrose wrote a manual titled *On the Duties of the Clergy*, which became one of his best-known books. In it, Ambrose identified the virtues necessary to succeed in ministry, including right speech, humility, modesty, faithfulness, and wisdom.

The first duty for clergy outlined by Ambrose was "to show due measure in the business of speaking" since it is "a true sacrifice of praise is offered to God."[27] Teachers, as James tells us, "will be judged with greater strictness" (James 3:1). Further, the tongue is a powerful tool for good, or evil, for with our tongue "we bless our Lord and Father, and with it we curse people who are made in the likeness of God" (James 3:9). Ambrose reiterated this by encouraging moderation in speech and spending time in silence. Those who teach and preach should know when to break silence and when to keep it. Because of their position of authority, the words that come from a preacher's mouth can bring life as well as destroy spirits. Indeed, pastors are called to speak with godly wisdom and authority that comes from God's word alone. Misspeaking, mishandling, and misapplying the word of God have grave consequences in the life of the church. While teachers of God's word should not be afraid to speak, they should also make sure to speak carefully and diligently.

Second, pastors must imitate the humility of Christ and the apostles. Referring to the humility of Christ described by Paul in Philippians 2, Ambrose declared, "We can see what a serious thing it is, then, to take anything away from a person when we ought to be sympathizing with him in his suffering, and how serious it is to act deceitfully and harmfully towards a person when we ought

---

27 Ambrose, *De Officiis*, trans. Ivor J. Davidson (Oxford: Oxford University Press, 2001), bk. 1, chap. 10, sec. 35.

to be offering him whatever service we can."[28] Further, a minister of the gospel should make "no claims for himself," take "no honours to himself," and expect "no immediate reward for whatever merits he has."[29] Ministry is primarily for the benefit of others. Thus, pastors should be first mindful of the needs of others. Indeed, to withhold ministry is to live contrary to the spirit of Christ. When pastors accept the shepherding role, they are accepting a call, as Paul describes to Titus, that is not "greedy for gain, but hospitable, a lover of good, self-controlled, upright, holy, and disciplined" (Titus 1:7–8). A pastor accepts the pastorate not for the honor of self, but for the sake of serving the church and the building up of others with the truth of God.

Third, pastors must exhibit modesty by practicing virtue for the sake of God's glory, not for the favor of people (a concept we also saw in Gregory of Nyssa). Regarding true virtue, Ambrose said that a happy life "does not court popular opinion as some kind of reward, nor is it afraid of it as a punishment. And so it is that the less it pursues glory, the more it rises above it."[30] Pastors seek God's glory, not their own. In this economy, the less Christian leaders seek their own glory, the more they glorify God. The quest for personal glory, according to Ambrose, "is a hindrance to eternal life," as seen, for example, in the religious leaders who already "received their reward" for their outward display of piety (Matt. 6:2, 5, 16).[31] The virtuous life of a pastor is one of a "secret spirituality," practicing things that contribute to Christian spiritual growth in a way that seeks God, not praise from others. Ambrose remarked,

28 Ambrose, *De Officiis* 3.3.19.
29 Ambrose, *De Officiis* 3.4.28.
30 Ambrose, *De Officiis* 2.1.2.
31 Ambrose, *De Officiis* 2.1.2.

We should never mutter a single word that is unjust even in our own heart, thinking to ourselves that it is hidden under a veil of silence; for the One who made the secret places hears words that are spoken in secret, and the One who implanted the power of thought in our innermost parts knows the hidden things which those innermost parts contain. So, as people who live under the eyes of their Judge, let us remember that everything we do is exposed to the light, and in this way it will be manifest to all.[32]

He also offered this illustration:

If you come across as someone who is always busy doing good works while you have a heart that lacks faith, it is as if you are trying to erect magnificent great domes on top of a building with a faulty foundation: the higher you raise the edifice, the greater its collapse will be, for without the support of faith no works can possibly last.[33]

Pastors proclaim eternal life or a God-directed life, one that is deeper than what any earthly happiness can provide. This happiness is understood in the depth of their souls. Thus, they practice what is good primarily for the sake of God's glory and in view of God, not self or others, though they hope that the congregation will follow their example.

Fourth, pastors must exhibit faithfulness. The good life is a pursuit of godly things for godly purposes, but this pursuit is not without its burdens and afflictions. Yet, said Ambrose, such "pains

32 Ambrose, *De Officiis* 2.19.96.
33 Ambrose, *De Officiis* 2.2.7.

and griefs are no obstacle to a happy life—they are in reality an advantage in discovering it."[34] To encourage the saints to persevere in faith, the apostle Peter stated,

> In this you rejoice, though now for a little while, if necessary, you have been grieved by various trials, so that the tested genuineness of your faith—more precious than gold that perishes though it is tested by fire—may be found to result in praise and glory and honor at the revelation of Jesus Christ. (1 Pet. 1:6–7)

The pastor must follow the pattern of Peter by encouraging the church to look to Jesus during trials and remember that virtue is refined in the fires of suffering. Trials are not hindrances to faithful Christian living; instead, they give it shape and significance. In fact, what we often consider to be the fruits of the good life—riches and abundance—are potential hindrances to the good life. Riches do not necessarily make one ungodly, but fascination with them detracts from godliness. Ambrose argued that Job and other biblical figures demonstrate how riches can coincide with godliness and yet how such joys are sharpened after enduring suffering.

Ambrose then went further to encourage pastors toward modeling everyday, habitual acts of faithfulness to Christ, stating, "We need to establish a kind of sequence and gradation covering everything we do, starting with familiar and ordinary actions and going right the way up to those that are truly outstanding."[35] God's people need to see common, ordinary acts of faithfulness, not monumental displays of spiritual grandeur. By exhibiting the

34 Ambrose, *De Officiis* 2.4.15.
35 Ambrose, *De Officiis* 2.7.28.

former, pastors model the nature of the Christian life in reality: moment-by-moment trust and obedience in the Lord.

Fifth, pastors must display wisdom and teach their congregations to be wise. Such pastoral advice is undergirded by the virtues of justice and prudence, which are from God. Dallas Willard, Christian philosopher and author, thus teaches that the pastor is someone who imparts true knowledge to his congregation. In his *Knowing Christ Today*, Willard described pastors as "the ones who, by profession at least, have the knowledge that must be taught to meet desperate human need."[36] Pastors, according to Willard, teach the nations to impart the healing knowledge of Christ. He continues,

> The task of Christian pastors and leaders is to present Christ's answers to the basic questions of life and to bring those answers forward as knowledge—primarily to those who are seeking and are open to following him, but also to all who may happen to hear, in the public arenas of a world in desperate need of knowledge of what is real and what is good.[37]

This knowledge of what is real and good is the knowledge of God and the virtues of Christ.

Paul tells us, "Whatever is true, whatever is honorable, whatever is just, whatever is pure, whatever is lovely, whatever is commendable, if there is any excellence, if there is anything worthy of praise, think about these things" (Phil. 4:8). All Christians are called to contemplate the things of God, indeed, God himself. Ambrose

---

36 Dallas Willard, *Knowing Christ Today: Why We Can Trust Spiritual Knowledge* (New York: HarperCollins, 2009), 197.

37 Willard, *Knowing Christ Today*, 198.

gave his readers a similar encouragement: "My sons, think before you act, and when you have thought long and hard do what you consider to be right. . . . Hold fast to all that is good."[38] This type of meditation affects the words we say and the actions we take. Pastoral wisdom thus comes from reflection on what is pure and lovely, which is God and his word.

Ambrose therefore concluded that the pastor "must present himself as model to others, as 'an example of good works, in doctrine, in purity, in seriousness of life'; his language must be wholesome and blameless; his advice beneficial, his life honourable, and his opinions seemly."[39] He asked, "How can you consider a man to be better than you when it comes to giving advice if you see that he is worse than you when it comes to morality?"[40] Pastors should therefore be diligent to support their advice with a good character and thus avoid muddling their wisdom with vice. Though the objective truth of the gospel stands forever, its veracity is enhanced and confirmed by the pastor's demeanor and way of life. Virtuous ministers understand the gravity of the knowledge they impart and the sacraments they promote, and they understand their own need for those very things.

Conclusion

Overall, Ambrose engaged the imaginations of his people by expounding the sacraments of the church, being driven by a pastoral concern to explain otherworldly realities to the common Christian. These mysteries of the faith are rooted in the grace of God and vital for the Christian life and ongoing growth. Ambrose thus teaches

---

38 Ambrose, *De Officiis* 2.30.153, 156.
39 Ambrose, *De Officiis* 2.17.86.
40 Ambrose, *De Officiis* 2.12.62.

us to take the sacramental nature of pastoral ministry seriously as stewards of God's grace. As we close, let us remember Ambrose's challenge regarding the spiritual power of God's truth:

> For what has more power than the confession of the Trinity which is daily celebrated by the mouth of the whole people? All eagerly vie one with the other in confessing the faith, and know how to praise in verse the Father, Son, and Holy Spirit. So they all have become teachers, who scarcely could be disciples.[41]

---

41 Ambrose, *Sermon Against Auxentius*, sec. 34 in *St. Ambrose: Select Works and Letters*, trans. H. de Romestin, E. de Romestin, and H. T. F. Duckworth, 2:10 (New York: Christian Literature, 1896), 436.

4

The Skilled Pastor and Origen of Alexandria

If there is some secret and hidden thing of God we long to know . . . let us faithfully and humbly inquire into the more concealed judgments of God that are sown in the Holy Scriptures.

ORIGEN OF ALEXANDRIA

Do your best to present yourself to God as one approved, a worker who has no need to be ashamed, rightly handling the word of truth.

2 TIMOTHY 2:15

WE (COLEMAN AND SHAWN) often feel like we live in two different worlds: one of ministry and one of academia. These worlds are filled with people who have spiritual needs and intellectual questions. Part of our calling is to train, equip, and provide spiritual care to the church. We also teach college and seminary students Scripture, theology, church history, ministry, and spiritual disciplines. Here is where these two worlds meet: when academics support the church and the church supports academics. We want to see the academy thrive in the depth of the Christian intellectual tradition but also grow and maintain a deep concern for ministry to the church and ministerial training. Similarly, we want to see the local church as a kingdom outpost for theologically, historically, and biblically informed gospel proclamation, racial reconciliation, poverty alleviation, and human flourishing. The church is not a place for anti-intellectualism, nor is the academy the sole locale for intellectual pursuits. We want the church and the academy to live in a rightly ordered relationship.[1]

Because of this, we believe that the pastor is a local theologian and must cultivate intellectual depth. This does not mean he must become an academic but that he must embark on an exploration of the Christian tradition, Christian theology, and the Christian Scriptures. Indeed, every pastor is a theologian for their congregation. Our hope in this chapter is to promote such adventure and explain why it is a major component of the pastoral life. We do not want less Bible in the pastor's life but more. We do not want less theology; we want more. And we want more of the classical tradition as well. The qualities of a learner can and should mark the minister.

When was the last time you read a book that stretched your thinking, read a passage of Scripture that pressed your methodological skills, or were asked a question you struggled to answer? What

---

1   See the Center for Pastor Theologians (http://www.pastortheologians.com), which seeks to support this goal. For more on their vision to practice "ecclesial theology," see Gerald Hiestand and Todd A. Wilson, *The Pastor Theologian: Resurrecting an Ancient Vision* (Grand Rapids, MI: Zondervan, 2015).

was your response afterward? Did you move on with your life or dig deeper and seek further training? A pastor need not become an academic but he should exhibit excellence in his office.

Pastors as Theologians

But if a pastor is to be a theologian, and a theologian a pastor, what is the difference between them? According to Kevin Vanhoozer, theologians are ministers of understanding and pastors are ministers of service. Theologians labor to understand the depths of theology, and pastors serve the church to help people understand.[2] As we saw in chapter 2 on the spirituality of the pastor according to Gregory of Nyssa, theology is contemplative reflection on God and all things in relation to God and leads to the spiritual formation of the people of God. Thus, theology is to serve as a conduit of life for the local church. By using theology, pastors provide a shepherding, leading, teaching, nurturing, and soul-caring ministry to the local church. Yes, they sometimes need to know how to make a budget, change a lightbulb, or troubleshoot a computer. But first and foremost, a pastor cares for the people of God and contemplates the theological realities of God for his people and their benefit.

How many of us have been taught that 2 Timothy 2:15 refers to giving a precise reading of the Scriptures? This passage says, "Do your best to present yourself to God as one approved, a worker who has no need to be ashamed, rightly handling the word of truth." Certainly, rightly handling Scripture includes offering a

---

2   "Pastors are called not to practice academic theology but to minister theological understanding, helping people to interpret the Scriptures, their cultures, and their own lives in relation to God's great work of redemption summed up *in Christ*." Kevin J. Vanhoozer and Owen Strachan, *The Pastor as Public Theologian: Reclaiming a Lost Vision* (Grand Rapids, MI: Baker Academic, 2015), 112.

sound interpretation. However, it is more than this. This phrase conveys the sense of making a road clear and displaying proper virtue. Thus, to divide the Scriptures rightly includes a pursuit of virtue in the one who offers a sound interpretation. Pastors must have patience, winsomeness, courage, and the ability to teach the Scriptures clearly. They must embody peace, correct opponents, and be able to teach (2 Tim. 2:20–26).

Yet, the church must also have the ability to understand and perform the scriptural witness that the pastor communicates to them. Thus, pastors must also encourage virtue in their hearers (2 Tim. 2:14). They are to ward off irreverent talk and babble and lead the people of God toward greater godliness (2 Tim. 2:16–19).

When I (Coleman) train students for ministry and converse with peers who labor in ministry, I understand that not everyone can give the same amount of time to reading and learning. Not all have the same interests, desires, and callings. You will never find me on a golf course. Some pastors may love a good volume of Bavinck, while others would rather read a mystery novel. Yet, regardless of how we are wired, we must all cultivate Christlike virtue in our study of Scripture and also seek to hone our soul care skills.

Virtuous Exegesis

So what exactly is the role of virtue before and during one's reading of Scripture? Unlike our modern education system, training in ethics preceded training in reading, understanding, analysis, and teaching in the era of the church fathers. Why? Because they believed that a student had to become a certain kind of person before he could proceed with higher levels of learning and understanding.[3]

---

3   See the works of Pierre Hadot, who shows how philosophy was a way of life during the time of the church fathers: Michael Chase, trans., *Philosophy as a Way of Life* (Oxford: Blackwell,

For the fathers, the pursuit of virtue preceded the pursuit of skills (exegetical, theological, or pastoral). Thus, ministerial ethics was not just one class (if that!) in a seminary curriculum; it *was* the curriculum. This shows us that by giving proper attention to our training's telos, we can cultivate virtue in our lives and subsequently become better ministers to the church. As we saw in Basil, Gregory of Nyssa, and Ambrose, contemplating God and diligently pursuing virtue serve as essential criteria for good reading and proper interpretation of Scripture.

When it comes to rightly handling the Scriptures, perhaps the most important virtue to cultivate is humility, what we might call hermeneutical humility. What kind of reader should one be while reading the Bible?[4] A virtuous and humble reader. Though pastors should possess elementary abilities in biblical languages and history, hermeneutical methods, and theology, they must remember that their character also informs how they read Scripture passages. When approaching Scripture, humility is key because one is approaching the word of God. But what does this mean? Think of how you display humility with your friends, family, peers, or

---

1995) and *What Is Ancient Philosophy?* (Cambridge, MA: Harvard University Press, 2002). For example, Hadot comments on the role of virtue in the process of reading: "Moreover, each commentary was considered a spiritual exercise—not only because the search for the meaning of a text really does demand the moral qualities of modesty and love for the truth, but also because the reading of each philosophical text was supposed to produce a transformation in the person reading or listening to the commentary." Hadot, *What Is Ancient Philosophy?*, 155.

4 Richard Briggs asks a similar question: "What sort of reader should one be in order to read the Bible? I have come to think that this question is at least as important as the perennial question of how we should read the Bible, but equally I have not wanted to give up on the notion that scriptural texts will have their own particular contribution to make toward one's reflection on the question of what sort of reader one should be." Richard Briggs, *The Virtuous Reader: Old Testament Narrative and Interpretive Virtue*, Studies in Theological Interpretation (Grand Rapids, MI: Baker Academic, 2010), 9.

parishioners—you hear them out, give deference as needed, and refrain from displaying condescension or haughtiness.

This kind of humility also includes certain methods of reading. What we call "hermeneutical humility" is similar to what Vanhoozer labels "interpretive virtue," which he defines as, "a disposition of the mind and heart that arises from the motivation for understanding, for cognitive contact with the meaning of the text."[5] Vanhoozer sets forth four additional interpretive virtues: honesty, openness, attention, and obedience.[6] These virtues assist readers of Scripture in their exegesis.

Soul Care Skills

In addition to cultivating virtues like hermeneutical humility, pastors must seek to hone their soul care skills. Soul care is patiently supporting people's flourishing by helping them know God, understand how they are known by him, and lay bare all the needs of their soul before him, the one who nurtures and mends the brokenness of humanity. Henri Nouwen says,

> Spiritual formation . . . is not about steps or stages on the way to perfection. It's about the *movements* from the mind to the heart through prayer in its many forms that reunite us with God, each other, and our truest selves. . . . Prayer is standing in the presence of God with the mind in the heart—that is, in the point of our being where there are no divisions or distinctions and where we are totally one within ourselves, with God, and with others and the whole creation.[7]

5   Kevin J. Vanhoozer, *Is There a Meaning in This Text? The Bible, the Reader, and the Morality of Literary Knowledge* (Grand Rapids, MI: Zondervan, 1998), 376.

6   Vanhoozer, *Is There a Meaning in This Text?*, 377.

7   Henri Nouwen, *Spiritual Formation: Following the Movements of the Spirit* (New York: HarperOne, 2010), xvii.

Thus the aim of soul care is to mature the inner person. It provides space and awareness of humanity's internal chaos and turmoil and aids a person in becoming whole and abiding with God. Let's now look at a few examples of skillful soul care—understanding the human condition, applying the right medicine, and not neglecting to care for ourselves.

UNDERSTAND THE HUMAN CONDITION

In our (Shawn's and Coleman's) experience, many faithful Christians struggle to understand how the gospel influences their everyday life. Jerry Bridges, in *Transforming Grace*, exhorts Christians to preach the gospel to themselves daily.[8] The gospel is a redemptive message of infinite proportions. It does not just save you once. It perpetually redeems, rescues, and sanctifies all of who you are. The gospel is a story of the victory of God as the Father begets his Son to redeem humanity by the Spirit.

While we care for souls, we must remember the implications of the incarnation. God the Son entered the human realm, took on human nature, and redeemed all creation, which was subjected to death. The Son had to be human to redeem humanity. All that the Son assumed in his human nature, he redeemed.[9] His redemption is more than just a get-out-of-hell-free card: it is a cosmic reality touching the very fabric of creation, including every cell of our body and every crevice of our soul.

Here are some telltale signs that we need redemption. When it comes to idols of the heart, do you sin when you have it, sin when

---

8   Jerry Bridges, *Transforming Grace* (Carol Stream, IL: NavPress, 2016).
9   See St. Gregory of Nazianzus, *Epistle* 101.5 in *On God and Christ: The Five Theological Orations and Two Letters to Cledonius*, trans. Frederick Williams and Lionel Wickham, Popular Patristics Series 23 (Crestwood, NY: St Vladimir's Seminary Press, 2002).

you lose it, and sin to keep it? In considering the pains and spiritual needs of the soul, we must traverse well beyond the first and second layers of spiritual concerns to excavate anxieties that reside deeper in—far closer to the inner core of one's identity. Soul care focuses on the inward, invisible features of one's soul with the goal of drawing out what is hidden and displaying Christian virtue. It is a movement of inward introspection that will lead to an outward showcase of Christlike virtue. Henri Nouwen writes, "Spiritual formation presents opportunities to enter into the center of our heart and become familiar with the complexities of our own inner life."[10] Here are a few questions to consider when guiding someone through this process:

1. What are you most afraid of in this situation and why?
2. What is causing you to not embrace God or feel embraced by God in these hardships and why?
3. Why do you joke about painful memories? What are you afraid to express?
4. Do you think that God is pleased with or disappointed in you and why do you think that?

You could also do a similar exercise with a fellow Christian by asking one another, What do you fear the most and why? Is it dying? Dying alone, dying slowly, feeling death, turning fifty and not having your children or spouse love you? What specifically is it about this that you fear? Then place the beauty of Jesus before one another. Feel free to sit together for some time, chasing the inner core of your identity and examining how these fears dwell within you.

10 Nouwen, *Spiritual Formation*, vii.

After this (often scary and exhausting) exercise, you should both come to a similar conclusion: the gospel of God and the beauty of Jesus perpetually redeem our core identity, our most authentic self. We affirm what David Benner asserts: "People who have never developed a deep personal knowing of God will be limited in the depth of the personal knowing of themselves."[11] The gospel of God not only saves you but redeems and rescues all of you and brings clarity to who you truly are. Jesus frees and rescues you. Jesus frees and rescues your relationships.

APPLY THE RIGHT MEDICINES

On the cover of an older edition of Thomas Watson's *All Things for Good* in the Banner of Truth's Puritan Paperback series is a spoon and a vial of liquid medicine.[12] This image conveyed the message that Watson declared inside:

> All things work together for good. This expression "work together" refers to medicine. Several poisonous ingredients put together, being tempered by the skill of the apothecary, make a sovereign medicine, and work together for the good of the patient. So all God's providences being divinely tempered and sanctified, do work together for the best to the saints.[13]

Thus some have called pastors the physicians of the soul—those who administer the medicine of Christ to sick souls in the local church. Just like the work of medicine, the work of soul care

---

11 David G. Benner, *The Gift of Being Yourself: The Sacred Call of Self-Discovery* (Downers Grove, IL: Intervarsity, 2015), 27.

12 Thomas Watson, *All Things for Good*, Puritan Paperbacks (Carlisle, PA: Banner of Truth, 1986).

13 Watson, *All Things for Good*, 5.

requires much labor, skill, and patience. Suppose one person needs penicillin for their health concerns but a different person is allergic to penicillin. I (Coleman) think about my father, who spent forty-seven years as a pharmacist. These skilled workers must know how drugs affect people and their ailments. They must also understand the nuances of dosage and application (e.g., topical, oral) in order to administer the proper care. Though a medical doctor signs the prescription, the pharmacist is held liable if a drug is mislabeled or the incorrect dosage is given to a patient. The life and livelihood of a person is in their hands. A pharmacist must know their patient well in order to dispense life-giving treatment and prevent the use of life-damaging poison. Similarly, a minister must discern both the kind of spiritual medicine that is needed by a particular person as well as how to administer it.

Gregory the Great used this medicinal metaphor when describing the act of preaching. He concluded this discussion by saying, "The discourse of the teacher should be adapted to the character of his audience so that it can address the specific needs of each individual and yet never shrink from the art of communal edification."[14] In other words, while a similar outcome is required for each person, the means to accomplish that outcome might differ.

The local church includes a diverse array of attendees, and the minister should know how to relate to them all. He must be adept at reading people well. Like a pharmacist, the pastor must dispense the proper spiritual dosage to each specific soul. First Thessalonians 5:14 says, "We urge you, brothers, admonish the idle, encourage the fainthearted, help the weak, be patient with them all." Though the intended outcome is still the same—complete sanctification

14 St. Gregory the Great, *The Book of Pastoral Rule*, trans. George E. Demacopoulos, Popular Patristics Series 34 (Crestwood, NY: St. Vladimir's Seminary Press, 2007), bk. 1, sec. 1.

(1 Thess. 5:23)—three different kinds of people require three different kinds of medicine.

I (Shawn) was in my early twenties when first hired as an associate pastor. Reflecting on those years, I remember several mistakes as well as many blessed times. The people I served were a delight to be around—probably because three-quarters of this church consisted of people seventy-five to eighty-five-years old. I was in my early twenties, pastoring people who could be my great-grandparents. Some were beyond generous with me. Some were quite grumpy with me. Some were joyful and had story after story of how the Lord had been kind to them in their difficult life journey. Some could not seem to find any form of joy in their life.

I learned several things. Most importantly, this experience taught me how to engage and shepherd people much older than me. First Timothy 4–5 and Titus 2 were my anchors in that season. In 1 Timothy 5:1–2, we are encouraged to minister to four different kinds of people: older men, older women, younger men, and younger women: "Do not rebuke an older man but encourage him as you would a father, younger men as brothers, older women as mothers, younger women as sisters, in all purity." The Bible calls us to minister to all our people according to their season of life. You do not minister to a twenty-year-old in the same way you minister to a forty, sixty, or eighty-year-old. Moreover, you will minister differently to a sixty-year-old mature, godly woman than you would to a spiritually immature man of the same age. Many of us still need to grow in how we minister to diverse cultures and ethnicities.[15] Overall, ministers must labor to know the kinds of people in their congregations and exhort, teach, and lead them

15   See Jarvis J. Williams, *Redemptive Kingdom Diversity: A Biblical Theology of the People of God* (Grand Rapids, MI: Baker Academic, 2021); Jamaal E. Williams and Timothy Paul Jones,

accordingly. While the destination of all believers will be quite similar, the manner in which you influence and lead them may be quite different. Here is a quick exercise you can try in order to improve in this area: Look at your church directory. Can you name one to two spiritual needs of each person that reflect their current life circumstances? If you struggle to remember who everyone is, try making flash cards with pictures of members and their names on one side and specific prayer requests on the other.

CARE FOR YOUR OWN SOUL

As a pastor it is easy to forget to tend to one's own soul. We have regrettably met many pastors who have neglected their needs. We too have had seasons of soul neglect and are only met with grief and anxiety as a result. Ministry is week in and week out, and endless people and tasks vie for your time. Time itself feels like an ever-present enemy to the spiritual life of the minister. As we explained in chapter 2, the spiritual life of a pastor is of utmost importance. Regrettably, it too often gets shoved to the bottom of the ministry to-do list.

But the Bible shows us a different way. Let's consider the image presented in Psalm 42 of a deer thirsting for water, which conjures the feeling of serenity that is found in the mountains. Yosemite National Forest is a yearly to biyearly vacation spot for me (Shawn) and my family. Often, we watch deer walk across the meadows with peace. They walk alone or in a small pack and drink from the cold brook. Regrettably I (Coleman) do not have access to anything resembling a mountain in north Texas, but there are still plenty of deer around to observe. In our neighborhood, there is a big nature trail where many deer reside. On family walks, we frequently spot a deer or two in the

---

In Church as It Is in Heaven: Cultivating a Multiethnic Kingdom Culture (Downers Grove, IL: Intervarsity, 2023).

woods. I often consider how these deer coexist amid the hustle and bustle of suburban life with SUVs shuttling kids to soccer practice and Chick-fil-A serving up endless chicken sandwiches and fries. These creatures are unconcerned with the caffeinated anxieties of our modern life. Though they witness what goes on around them, they experience a simplicity that we cannot seem to attain.

When was the last time you prayed simply for the sake of enjoying time with God like the deer in Psalm 42? We are speaking about something different from praying in preparation for delivering a sermon, lesson, or counseling session. Sometime this week, clear a spot in your calendar to spend time envisioning yourself as a deer. Travel alone or with a small group of intimate friends and long for God without the pressures to perform. Intimacy with God is not a task on a checklist. Does your soul thirst for the refreshing reprieve found in the presence of God? We see that the psalmist's tears are grief and loneliness in light of the seeming absence of God (Ps. 42:3). But even a downcast soul is a fertile place to be refreshed in God (Ps. 42:5). Whether in peace or anxiety, our restoration comes from abiding with God.

Overall, we encourage you to find meaningful times of retreat for your own soul. Find rest in God and develop skills to minister to yourself. Walk in a field to pray and feel joy. Take a nap if you are exhausted. By doing these, you lead the way in your local community to a healthy spiritual life.

Origen of Alexandria

Origen of Alexandria (c. 186–255) is a wonderful example for this kind of skilled pastor because he engaged with both the academy and church. He is often associated with apocryphal stories of cutting off limbs and teaching heresy, and it is true that he is quite a polarizing figure. Yet, most have probably heard more about his views than actually read his writings. Though he was not an ordained pastor, he mentored fellow believers and contributed greatly to the field of exegesis.[16] Beryl Smalley argues, "To write a history of Origenist influence on the west would be tantamount to writing a history on western exegesis."[17] Even after a canonical condemnation in 543 (at the Second Council of Constantinople), Origen was so influential as a philologist, exegete, and theologian that it proved quite difficult to ignore his ideas. John McGuckin says,

> Of course, all of the greatest thinkers of the patristic age were in his debt, and even after his condemnation he was too deeply inserted into the fabric of Christian theologizing ever to be dismissed or forgotten. He had been the founding architect (as far as its international reception was concerned) of biblical commentary as a mode of organizing Christian reflection, and no one who took the Bible seriously in the first millennium of the church was able to avoid his groundbreaking writing.[18]

The influence of Origen's work on both biblical interpretation and theological reflection was far-reaching. Origen, "having commented on every aspect of canonical Scripture . . . left behind such a vast and pervasive body of work that from it would be derived thereafter the foundation for all teachings of the Church," which led Gregory of Nazianzus to say, "Origen is the whetstone of us all."[19]

---

16 Ronald E. Heine, *Origen: Scholarship in the Service of the Church*, Christian Theology in Context (Oxford: Oxford University Press, 2010), 60–61.

17 Beryl Smalley, *The Study of the Bible in the Middle Ages* (Oxford: Basil Blackwell, 1952), 14.

18 John Anthony McGuckin, "The Scholarly Works of Origen," in *Origen*, ed. John Anthony McGuckin, The Westminster Handbooks to Christian Theology (Louisville, KY: Westminster John Knox, 2004), 26.

19 Suda, Ὠριγένης 182.

Details of Origen's childhood, education, early Christian piety, and life in Alexandria were kept by the historian Eusebius of Caesarea (ca. 260–339). Origen was raised in Alexandria and thoroughly educated in Greek and the Scriptures. His father, Leonides, suffered martyrdom in 202 during Septimius Severus's persecution.[20] According to Eusebius, Origen was devoted to God even at a young age during the rise of persecution in Alexandria. Eusebius explained, "It will not be out of place to describe briefly how deliberately the boy's mind was set on the Divine Word from that early age."[21] Elsewhere he wrote, "When, therefore, the flame of persecution was kindled to a fierce blaze, and countless numbers were being wreathed with the crowns of martyrdom, Origen's soul was possessed with such a passion for martyrdom, while he was still quite a boy."[22]

When Origen heard of his father's imprisonment, he rushed to locate his clothes. Yet, his mother hid them, thus sparing his life. Out of modesty, he chose to stay home rather than rush headlong to his father's side. Eusebius commented, "Let this be recorded as the first proof of Origen's boyish readiness of mind and genuine love of godliness."[23]

According to Eusebius, Origen's father urged him "before beginning his Ἑλληνικῶν [pagan studies] lessons to train himself in sacred studies, exacting from him each day learning by heart and repetition."[24] Eusebius continued,

His father would rebuke him ostensibly to his face, counseling him to seek nothing beyond his years nor anything further than

---

20 Eusebius, *Eusebius: Ecclesiastical History, Volume II: Books 6-10*, trans. J. E. L. Oulton, Loeb Classical Library 265 (Cambridge, MA: Harvard University Press, 1932).

21 Eusebius, *Ecclesiastical History*, bk. 6, chap. 1.

22 Eusebius, *Ecclesiastical History*, bk. 6, chap. 2, sec. 3.

23 Eusebius, *Ecclesiastical History* 6.2.6.

24 Eusebius, *Ecclesiastical History* 6.2.8.

the manifest meaning; but secretly in himself he rejoiced greatly, and gave profound thanks to God, the Author of all good things, that He had deemed him worthy to be the father of such a boy.[25]

Origen never became a bishop, but he did join the Alexandrian school and perform pastoral duties. Overall, Eusebius presented Origen as an ideal and virtuous teacher who would visit Christians before their martyrdom. Eusebius wrote,

He was present not only with the holy martyrs who were in prison, not only with those who were under examination right up to the final sentence, but also when they were being led away afterwards to their death, using great boldness and coming to close quarters with danger; so that, as he courageously drew near and with great boldness greeted the martyrs with a kiss.[26]

Surely Origen is a model for the skilled pastor. Let's look now at some notable features of his skill as an exegete and philologist that are worthy of emulation by pastors today.

The Good Reader

Scattered through Origen's writings are descriptions of the kind of person who can read the Scriptures well. In modern hermeneutics, reading well is often defined as reading objectively. Attention is usually given to the interpretive methods used to gauge the accuracy of readings. But, as we noted earlier in our discussion of hermeneutical humility, reading well is directly related to the reader's character and his posture toward the Scriptures in patristic exegesis. The

25 Eusebius, *Ecclesiastical History* 6.2.10–11.
26 Eusebius, *Ecclesiastical History* 6.3.4.

moral state of the reader, the skills and abilities of the reader, and the outcome of the reader's interpretation for the community were of primary importance to early Christians.[27]

In Origen's descriptions of good readers, he had much to say about the first point. First, in his *Commentary on Romans*, Origen highlighted several exegetical virtues to cultivate and vices to avoid, writing,

> If there is some secret and hidden thing of God we long to know
> . . . let us faithfully and humbly inquire into the more concealed
> judgments of God that are sown in the Holy Scriptures. Surely
> this is also why the Lord was saying, "Search the Scriptures!"
> (Jn 5:39) since he knew that these things are opened not by
> those who fleetingly listen to or read [the Scriptures] while oc-
> cupied with other business, but by those who with an upright
> and sincere heart search more deeply into the Holy Scriptures,
> by constant effort and uninterrupted nightly vigils. I know well
> that I myself am not one of these. But if anyone seeks in this
> way, he will find.[28]

According to Origen, exegetes must be faithful, humble, upright, and sincere instead of being preoccupied with other things.

Second, in his *Letter to Gregory*, Origen exhorted Bishop Gregory Thaumaturgus to be attentive and devoted to exegesis, alluding to Paul's advice in 1 Timothy 4:13. He wrote,

---

27 See Martens, who highlights how early Christian authors envisioned the ideal interpreter: Peter W. Martens, "Ideal Interpreters," in *The Oxford Handbook of Early Christian Biblical Interpretation*, ed. Paul M. Blowers and Peter W. Martens (Oxford: Oxford University Press, 2019), 149–65.

28 Peter Martens, *Origen and Scripture: The Contours of the Exegetical Life*, Oxford Early Christian Studies (Oxford: Oxford University Press, 2012), 177n67.

Now you, my lord and son, attend principally to the reading of the divine writings. For we who read the divine writings are in need of great attentiveness, lest we say or think something too rashly about them. And devoting yourself to the reading of the divine books with a disposition faithful and pleasing to God, knock at its closed door and it will be opened to you by the doorkeeper of whom Jesus said: "To this one the doorkeeper opens" (John 10:3). And as you apply yourself to this divine reading, seek correctly with an unshaken faith in God the meaning of the divine writings hidden from the multitude. Do not be satisfied with knocking and seeking, for prayer is most necessary for understanding the divine books.[29]

In other words, Gregory must have a disposition that is pleasing to God, not be satisfied with knowing and seeking (John 10:3), and accompany reading with prayer because it is necessary to understand the Scriptures.

Last, Origen also spoke about the virtues of his patron, Ambrose:

Although he thinks that I am industrious and exceedingly thirsty for the divine word, he has put [me] to shame with his own zeal and his love for the sacred disciplines . . . For it is neither possible to eat without conversation, nor, after having eaten, to take a walk and allow the body to rest awhile, but even during these times we are compelled to study and to correct the copies; nor indeed are we allowed to go to bed for the whole night in order to care for the body, since study extends deep into the night. If I were permitted to say, [we do] these things from daybreak until

29 Martens, *Origen and Scripture*, 172.

the ninth, and at times, even the tenth hour. For all those who desire to labor devote these periods of time to the examination of the divine words and their readings.[30]

Ambrose was a good reader because he was passionate about God's word.

Philology for the Church

In addition to being a good reader, Origen was also a good philologist and used his skill for the good of the church. Too often, Christians today downplay the importance of biblical languages for interpreting Scripture, engaging in theological discourse, and preaching. But studying the biblical languages is a task good in and of itself and contributes greatly to ministry. Even Augustine, who struggled to maintain skills in Greek and Hebrew, once said,

> The great remedy for ignorance . . . is knowledge of languages. And men who speak the Latin tongue, of whom are those I have undertaken to instruct, need two other languages for the knowledge of Scripture, Hebrew and Greek, that they may have recourse to the original texts if the endless diversity of the Latin translators throw them into doubt.[31]

In other words, philology helps us to better understand the Scriptures.

Origen clearly believed this. Few before him had tried to write Bible commentaries but he produced thirteen books on Genesis,

30 Martens, *Origen and Scripture*, 177.
31 Augustine, *Saint Augustine: On Christian Teaching*, trans. R. P. H. Green, Oxford World's Classics (Oxford: Oxford University Press, 1997), bk. 2, sec. 11.

thirty-six on Isaiah, twenty-five on Ezekiel, twenty-five on the
Minor Prophets, thirty-five on the Psalms, three on Proverbs, ten
on the Song of Songs, five on Lamentations, and several on the
New Testament, all informed by philology.[32] He also produced the
Hexapla, a comparison of the Hebrew Old Testament and Greek
versions of the text, with accompanying Greek transliterations of
the Hebrew. According to Eusebius,

> So accurate was the examination that Origen brought to bear
> upon the divine books, that he even made a thorough study of
> the Hebrew tongue, and got into his own possession the origi-
> nal writings in the actual Hebrew characters, which were extant
> among the Jews. Thus, too, he traced the editions of the other
> translators of the sacred writings besides the Seventy; and besides
> the beaten track of translations, that of Aquila and Symmachus
> and Theodotion, he discovered certain others, which were used
> in turn, which, after lying hidden for a long time, he traced and
> brought to light, I know not from what recesses. With regard to
> these on account of their obscurity (not knowing whose in the
> world they were) he merely indicated this: that the one he found
> at Nicopolis, near Actium, and the other in such another place. At
> any rate, in the Hexapla of the Psalms, after the four well-known
> editions, he placed beside them not only a fifth but also a sixth
> and a seventh translation; and in the case of one of these he has
> indicated again that it was found at Jericho in a jar in the time
> of Antoninus the Son of Severus. All these he brought together,
> dividing them into clauses and placing them one over against the

32 Fred Norris, "Origen," in *The Early Christian World*, ed. Philip F. Esler (London: Routledge,
   2000), 1010–11; Joseph T. Lienhard, "Origen and the Crisis of the Old Testament in the
   Early Church," *Pro Ecclesia* 9, no. 3 (2000): 362–63.

other, together with the actual Hebrew text; and so he has left us the copies of the Hexapla, as it is called. He made a further separate arrangement of the edition of Aquila and Symmachus and Theodotion together with that of the Seventy, in the Tetrapla.[33]

Origen's feat was incredible, and it gives us a good example of how Christians in ages past devoted themselves to the study of Scripture from all angles. In his *Letter to Julius Africanus*, Origen affirmed this point, saying of his Hexapla that

> I make it my endeavor not to be ignorant of their various readings, so that in my controversies with the Jews I may avoid quoting to them what is not found in their copies, and also may be able to make positive use of what is found there, even when it is not to be found in our scriptures. If we are prepared for our discussions with them in this way, they will no longer be able, as so often happens, to laugh scornfully at Gentile believers for their ignorance of the true reading, which they have.[34]

Even in the third century, Origen worked through textual variants and desired to be aware of them in order to answer people's questions about the Scriptures more effectively. In fact, in the Hellenistic classroom, students had to work through four philological exercises: (1) text-critical analysis, (2) oral recitation of a passage, (3) literary and historical analysis, and (4) aesthetic and moral evaluation. Under literary and historical analysis, there were four additional sets of inquiries: (1) the meaning of words,

---

33 Oulton, *Eusebius*, 6.16.
34 Maurice F. Wiles, "Origen as Biblical Scholar," in *The Cambridge History of the Bible*, ed. P. R. Ackroyd and C. F. Evans (Cambridge: Cambridge University Press, 1970), 456.

(2) grammatical and rhetorical analysis, (3) metrical evaluation and style, and (4) historical evaluation.[35]

Though many of us will never receive this kind of education or attain to the level of Origen when it comes to our linguistic skills, we need to learn the importance of acquiring such skills for the task of rightly interpreting Scripture for the people of God. As we've already shown, every soul is unique, so we need to offer tailored soul care. Further, Scripture is complicated, leading our people to ask many difficult questions, so we need skill in thinking through big ideas. Origen's story, while extraordinary in many ways, provides a good model for us. His rigor calls for excellence in the languages and textual criticism and reminds us to support, not detract from, a pastor's work in philology.

Conclusion

Though the task of becoming a skilled pastor looms large, we should not be overwhelmed but rather humbled that God desires to use our words and work to bring life to his people. Along the way, we grow in our understanding of our people and their needs, including the burdens they bear. We refresh our people from the rivers of God's life as we, like the deer drinking from its flowing streams, grow in our dependence upon him and his power. Thus, the skilled pastor is one who relies not on his own virtue or skills but on the power that lies behind the beauty of that virtue and the proper and timely use of those skills.

---

35 For more information on ancient literary criticism and the training that early Christians received, see Martens, *Origen and Scripture*, 41–42; Martin Irvine, *The Making of Textual Culture: "Grammatica" and Literary Theory, 350–1100*, Cambridge Studies in Medieval Literature 19 (Cambridge: Cambridge University Press, 1994); R. Nünlist, *The Ancient Critic at Work: Terms and Concepts of Literary Criticism in Greek Scholia* (Cambridge: Cambridge University Press, 2009); Jaap Mansfeld, *Prolegomena: Questions to Be Settled Before the Study of an Author, or a Text*, Philosophia Antiqua 61 (Leiden: Brill, 1994).

PART 2

———————

THE THEOLOGICAL
VISION OF A PASTOR

5

The Biblical Pastor and Irenaeus of Lyons

What use is it to know the truth in words, only to defile the body and perform evil deeds? Or what profit indeed can come from holiness of body, if truth is not in the soul?

IRENAEUS OF LYONS

Pursue righteousness, godliness, faith, love, steadfastness, gentleness. Fight the good fight of the faith. Take hold of the eternal life to which you were called and about which you made the good confession in the presence of many witnesses.

I TIMOTHY 6:11–12

I (COLEMAN) GREW UP with a bifurcated view of the Bible. From sermons to youth group lessons, the message was as follows: the Old Testament gives us information about creation, God, and history, but it doesn't apply to us, and the New Testament is what really matters for our spiritual life. As a young adult entering seminary, I unconsciously brought this view along with me. I do not know when it clicked, but slowly, through studying and listening to lectures, I came to see that the Bible was one big story about redemption, and I had a part to play! A whole Bible, not just the twenty-seven books of the New Testament, was needed to understand all the beauty and profundity of the gospel. Only in modern times, primarily during the rise of biblical criticism in the nineteenth and twentieth centuries, was the Bible parsed out into demythologized kernels that were at best a system of morality and at worst the product of an oppressed people group. We had plenty of Bibles, but we had lost Scripture.[1]

This truncated view of Scripture, of course, is not how the Bible was read in the early church. The people of God have always seen the entire revealed word of God as the unique message of creation, fall, redemption, and consummation in light of the central figure of Jesus Christ. Though Scripture has been egregiously misapplied at various points in church history, it has always been the matrix of the Christian life. So we need to stop and consider: do we today have the same view of Scripture as Irenaeus and the early church? Is our worldview based on Scripture? Is knowing God through his Scripture our priority in preaching and discipleship? I can admit that throughout my ministry, I have not always thought as deeply about Scripture as I should have. There are times when the latest

---

1   For a helpful analysis of how the Bible became an academic text subject to critical scholarship at the expense of its function as Scripture for the community of God, see Michael Legaspi, *The Death of Scripture and the Rise of Biblical Studies* (Oxford, UK: Oxford University Press, 2010). Not only was the Bible dissected as a demythologized text but, as a result, the early church and its theology were scrutinized under the same critical lenses based on new, fashionable historiographical approaches that came to dominate the academy. For more on this issue see Andreas J. Köstenberger and Michael J. Kruger, *The Heresy of Orthodoxy: How Contemporary Culture's Fascination with Diversity Has Reshaped Our Understanding of Early Christianity* (Wheaton, IL: Crossway, 2010).

trend, ministry philosophy, or academic textbook occupied my mind and saturated my heart more than God's word. I remember that when I was a student minister, I was often more concerned about what tactics I could use to get students and families interested in our events and gatherings than I was about focusing on teaching Scripture. I also remember the rise of the smartphone and social media and how these shaped my ministry. It is not that I didn't care about the Bible and theology, but I often spent more time crafting social media posts and YouTube videos than I did on biblical meditation. Though I taught through Scripture, I spent too much mental energy considering ways to make my teaching sound catchy or relevant. There is no substitute for good rhetoric or timely application, but I was not always concerned with helping students see their place in the grand story of God's word and how Scripture is where we find true sustenance for our souls.

Being a biblical pastor requires us to consider how God's Spirit gives us what John J. O'Keefe and R. R. Reno call a "sanctified vision."[2] Do we see the Bible as just a good word for a Sunday morning or a grand word for all of life? Is Scripture a supplement for the occasional heartache or the vital transfusion to bring us back from the dead and sustain every cell of our spiritual life? Scripture truly is the "God-breathed" word, profitable for "teaching, for reproof, for correction, and for training in righteousness" (2 Tim. 3:16–17). Scripture is also the all-encompassing story of God's plan for all of creation.

Irenaeus of Lyons

Irenaeus of Lyons (130–202) is an excellent model of the biblical pastor. He was attuned to the depth and spiritual vitality of Scripture, the

---

2 See John J. O'Keefe and R. Reno, *Sanctified Vision: An Introduction to Early Christian Interpretation of the Bible* (Baltimore, MD: John Hopkins University Press, 2005).

lifeblood of the Christian. Robert Wilken observes, "For Irenaeus the Bible was a single narrative whose chief actor was God."[3] Irenaeus gives us our first blueprint for reading the Scriptures as one unified story about God and his redemptive work in Christ. Though this was the testimony of the apostles in the New Testament and even Jesus himself (Luke 24:13–35), Irenaeus was the first church father to systematize this interpretive scheme in order to address pastoral concerns of his day, and it had a massive influence on the Christian interpretation of Scripture in the early centuries. Wilken puts it this way:

> So successful was Irenaeus's approach to the interpretation of the Bible that it informed all later interpretation. Whether one reads Athanasius against Arius, Augustine against Pelagius, or Cyril of Alexandria against Nestorius, all assume that individual passages are to be read in light of the story that gives meaning to the whole.[4]

For Irenaeus, the idea that "Jesus Christ is the fulfillment of all things" informed all other "details of scripture."[5] Though we want to be sensitive to the genre, historical context, and literal sense of of Scripture, those are just the first of many layers contained in the God-breathed book we open in our laps.[6] Scripture shows both the historical accounts of God's work as well as the deeper spiritual realities of his kingdom. As Todd Billings argues, "The new world into which God brings us via Scripture is wide and spacious, but it

---

3   Robert Louis Wilken, *The Spirit of Early Christian Thought: Seeking the Face of God* (New Haven, CT: Yale University Press, 2003), 63.

4   Wilken, *Spirit of Early Christian Thought*, 68.

5   O'Keefe and Reno, *Sanctified Vision*, 37.

6   For more on the senses of Scripture as understood throughout church history see Keith D. Stanglin, *The Letter and Spirit of Biblical Interpretation: From the Early Church to Modern Practice* (Grand Rapids, MI: Baker Academic, 2018).

also has a specified character as a journey on a path of Jesus Christ by the power of the Spirit in anticipation of a transforming vision of the triune God."[7] Until we gain a sanctified vision of Scripture like Irenaeus and the fathers had, we will never be able to fully explore all the rich treasures contained in the word of God for the people of God.

Irenaeus, originally from Asia Minor, had sat under the teaching of Polycarp of Smyrna (69–155), a famous Christian martyr. Sadly, the life of Irenaeus was punctuated by persecution and bookended by moments of martyrdom. Yet, knowing and learning from people who were willing to die for their faith left a lasting impact on his spiritual life. Around 177, Irenaeus was present in Lyons when persecution was running rampant. After traveling to Rome to send a report of the persecution in Lyons, he returned to Lyons and immediately succeeded Pothinus as bishop. Though little additional biographical information exists regarding the remainder of Irenaeus's life and ministry, his surviving works reveal a deep concern for biblical doctrine and the spiritual maladies that arise from heresy. The fact that Irenaeus wrote in the heat of surrounding persecution heightens the significance of this point. Overall, he provided a pastoral theology for Christians in troubled times, focusing on the spiritual realities behind theological error in order to maintain an orthodox witness and an orthodox life. Concerned with theology just as much as morality, Irenaeus shows readers today the necessity of combatting error with faithful biblical teaching for the sake of remaining faithful to the faith "once for all delivered to the saints" (Jude 3).

In his book *Against Heresies*, Irenaeus exposed the danger of straying from orthodoxy by using the metaphor of a portrait. The

7   J. Todd Billings, *The Word of God for the People of God: An Entryway to the Theological Interpretation of Scripture* (Grand Rapids, MI: Eerdmans, 2005), 8.

Christian faith is like a jeweled portrait of a king, but those who twisted the faith according to their own whims reconstructed this portrait into one "of a dog or of a fox."[8] These scam artists then told onlookers "that the miserable likeness of the fox was, in fact, the beautiful image of the king."[9] But the jewels could only be assembled one way in order to produce an image of the king.

In this same spirit, D. Jeffrey Bingham says, "Church leaders who care for their congregations don't allow unacceptable thinking about the Trinity and Christ's person to go unchecked."[10] Pastors have a basic obligation to ensure their congregations are shaped by truth and not error and thus must remain vigilant in learning and imparting sound biblical doctrine. From Ivy League scholars to popular preachers to *New York Times* bestsellers, the truth of the gospel is questioned and deconstructed at every turn. Though Christians should not be surprised at this, pastors need to recognize the bombardment of error lobbied toward the church and equip believers to respond. Irenaeus models to Christians today the necessity of Christian doctrine as the antidote to pernicious error. Let's now look at one of his writings, *Demonstration of the Apostolic Teaching*, to catch a glimpse of how this pastor understood his task of passing on faithful biblical teaching.

The Importance of Orthodoxy

In short, *Demonstration* is a guide for how to read and receive the apostolic teaching. In one sense, Irenaeus was simply doing what others who came before him did: exhorting Christians to hold to

---

8   Irenaeus, *Against the Heresies*, trans. Dominic J. Unger, Ancient Christian Writers 55 (New York: Newman Press, 1992), bk. 1, chap. 8, sec. 1.

9   Irenaeus, *Against the Heresies* 1.8.1.

10   D. Jeffrey Bingham, *Pocket History of the Church* (Downers Grove, IL: InterVarsity, 2002), 52.

the teaching of the apostles regarding the gospel. Clement of Rome, Ignatius of Antioch, and the *Didache* all told readers to do the same thing. Even Justin Martyr told his non-Christian audience that "the memoirs" of the apostles were vitally important for Christian faith and practice.[11] So what made *Demonstration* unique? For its time, it was the longest and most comprehensive text setting forth the apostolic teaching for the sake of instructing Christians and thus came to serve as a catechetical tool for basic instruction in core Christian doctrine.

In *Demonstration*, Irenaeus's goal was to help readers understand biblical redemptive history and thus be able to combat false views that twisted the Scriptures. Christ is the key to reading Scripture and Irenaeus presented a clear and compelling case for this approach. In his text, Irenaeus was both demonstrating the proper way of reading the Bible and proving that Christ was the interpretive key to the biblical text.

Irenaeus began his *Demonstration* in a pastoral tone, writing to his friend Marcianus, who was zealous for the Lord to further increase his faith. He reminded Marcianus that holiness of life is important when approaching the holiness of Scripture, saying, "For what use is it to know the truth in words, only to defile the body and perform evil deeds?"[12] Here, Irenaeus was not only warning Marcianus of theological error but also exhorting him to faithful Christian living. For Irenaeus and other church fathers, heresy was not just theologically dangerous but led to spiritual and moral peril as well.

11 Leslie William Barnard, trans., *St. Justin Martyr, The First and Second Apologies*, Ancient Christian Writers 56 (Mahwah, NJ: Paulist Press, 1997).

12 John Behr, "Demonstration of the Apostolic Preaching," in *On the Apostolic Preaching*, St. Irenaeus of Lyons, Popular Patristics Series 17 (Crestwood, NY: St Vladimir's Seminary Press, 1997), preface, 2.

With this in mind, Irenaeus began the main body of his text by expositing the importance of the Christian doctrine of creation. Irenaeus understood that the Christian doctrine of creation was set apart from any other story of humanity's origin. He also understood that the tenets of God as creator of all things and humanity as his unique pinnacle of creative action were foundational doctrinal categories. Thus, he set out to show how God's word and Spirit were manifest from the beginning of creation. This also displayed God's triune nature. According to Irenaeus, the Father, Son, and Spirit are the three articles of faith, not as separate entities but as a full revelation of God as triune.

After Irenaeus unpacked the creation and fall narrative, which moved right into God's preparation for salvation and the work of redemption in Christ, his next task was to help readers see this plan of redemption in the Old Testament. He stated, "That all those things would thus come to pass was foretold by the Spirit of God through the prophets, that the faith of those who truly worship God might be certain in these things."[13] In the early church, the Old Testament was seen as Christian Scripture, a rich storehouse of Christological jewels.

After walking through how the Old Testament authors attested to the person and work of Christ, Irenaeus concluded, "This, beloved, is the preaching of the truth, and this is the character of our salvation, and this is the way of life, which the prophets announced and Christ confirmed and the apostles handed over and the Church, in the whole world, hands down to her children."[14] The phrase "handing over" or "handing down" describes the nature of pastoral

---

13 Irenaeus, *On the Apostolic Preaching*, trans. John Behr, Popular Patristics Series 17 (Crestwood, NY: St Vladimir's Seminary Press, 1997), 42.

14 Irenaeus, *On the Apostolic Preaching*, 298.

teaching and shepherding—the task of guarding the deposit of faith and faithfully expositing it for the church. Thus, pastoral shepherding was not a task of innovation but of preservation.

The Danger of Heresy

In addition to preserving orthodoxy, Irenaeus also warned of the dangers of heresy in his best-known work, *Against Heresies*. The original Greek title of this work translates as "On the detection and overthrow of knowledge falsely so called." In this book, Irenaeus sought to help readers understand heterodoxy for the sake of more fully understanding orthodoxy.

In the second century, various groups used the Bible for their own purposes, twisting it to fit their warped teaching. Irenaeus addressed these false teachers by name and systematically dissected their errors and flagrant misuse of Scripture. Some of the main offenders in Irenaeus's sights were Gnostic teachers Valentinus of Rome and Marcion of Sinope. In short, Marcion taught that Jesus Christ was an entirely new god compared to the god of Israel in the Old Testament. Whereas the god of Israel was vengeful and capricious, the god of the New Testament was one of compassion and benevolence. The Old Testament god was concerned only with lowly, physical things while the New Testament god was interested in higher, spiritual things. Hence, there was no fundamental unity between the Old and New Testaments. This led Marcion to reject the Old Testament and accept only a highly stylized and edited form of the New Testament, which included his version of the Gospel of Luke as well as select epistles of Paul. For Marcion, Paul was the only proper interpreter of Jesus's teaching; he rejected anything that smelled of Jewish influence.

Valentinus's views were similar, yet his interpretation of the Bible was filtered through a complicated cosmological web of higher and lower beings called Aeons. Like Marcion, Valentinus saw a radical disjunction between the Old and New Testament and believed that the account of creation and the experience of the early Israelites were written by misguided and mercurial individuals. For both Valentinus and Marcion, there was a high primal being who transcended all the muck and mire of human existence. True humanity was found in the spiritual domain, not the earthly, and the created world (including humanity) was the product of a lower being's rebellion. But in Valentinus's theology, there was hope for humanity. That hope lay in freeing the higher aspect of human beings by shedding away corporeal existence and attaching it to spiritual existence.

The lofty spiritual language of this Gnosticism was, and still is, quite attractive. The problem? It offers no true hope and is ultimately false. Irenaeus understood this well. At the beginning of his *Against Heresies* he stated,

> Error, in fact, does not show its true self, lest on being stripped naked it should be detected. Instead, it craftily decks itself out in an attractive dress, and thus, by an outward false appearance, presents itself to the more ignorant, truer than Truth itself, ridiculous as it is even to say this.[15]

Sin often looks too good to be true. Peel back the onion enough and you discover a rotten and gangrenous center. Irenaeus was concerned with the effects of Gnostic teachings not because he was looking to pick a fight but because he was looking to preserve souls.

---

15 Irenaeus, *Against the Heresies* 1.2.

The Guardrails of Orthodoxy

To preserve souls, pastors must stay between the guardrails of orthodoxy and test teaching that is potentially false. Irenaeus did this by using the rule of faith—an early creed of the church that summarized biblical doctrine. It provided a way to ensure that those who taught God's word did so correctly. Church historian J. N. D. Kelly notes that the

> second-century conviction that the "rule of faith" believed and taught in the Catholic Church had been inherited from the Apostles contains more than a germ of truth. Not only was the content of that rule, in all essentials, foreshadowed by the "pattern of teaching" accepted in the apostolic Church but its characteristic lineaments and outline found their prototypes in the confessions and credal summaries contained in the New Testament documents.[16]

Why use something like the rule of faith when you can simply preach the Bible and commend biblical doctrine? Because other so-called Christian groups claimed they were biblical too. It was not enough to preach the Bible; one had to do so correctly. Preaching and teaching was serious work, and the early church understood this. When confronted with groups peddling the gospel without its power and truth, leaders guided followers of Christ into truth and away from error by means of the rule. Its value was hermeneutical as well as pedagogical.

So what exactly did the rule say? Though its content was never solidified at a council or in writing, Irenaeus conveyed the essence

---

16 J. N. D. Kelly, *Early Christian Creeds*, 3rd ed. (New York: Continuum, 2006), 29.

of the apostolic message that guided the church and its teaching when he wrote that the church believes

> in one God the Father Almighty, the Creator of heaven and earth and the seas and all things that are in them; and in the one Jesus Christ, the Son of God, who was enfleshed for our salvation; and in the Holy Spirit, who through the prophets preached the Economies, the coming, the birth from a Virgin, the passion, the resurrection from the dead, and the bodily ascension into heaven of the beloved Son, Christ Jesus our Lord, and His coming from heaven in the glory of the Father to recapitulate all things, and to raise up all flesh of the whole human race, in order that to Christ Jesus, our Lord and God, Savior and King, according to the invisible Father's good pleasure, "every knee should bow [of those] in heaven and on earth and under the earth, and every tongue confess" Him, and that He would exercise just judgment toward all; and that, on the other hand, He would send into eternal fire the spiritual forces of wickedness, and the angels who transgressed and became rebels, and the godless, wicked, lawless, and blasphemous people; but, on the other hand, by bestowing life on the righteous and holy and those who kept His commandments and who have persevered in His love—both those who did so from the beginning and those who did so after repentance—He would bestow on them as a grace the gift of incorruption and clothe them with everlasting glory.[17]

Overall, this rule affirmed God as Trinity, Jesus as both God and man, and his virgin birth, crucifixion, resurrection, ascension, and

---

17 Irenaeus, *Against the Heresies* 1.10.1.

future return to judge evil and reward righteousness. The rule filtered out heretical teaching and promoted biblical truth, claiming that the bodily birth, life, resurrection, ascension, and return of Jesus Christ were essential to gospel proclamation. A century before Irenaeus, the apostle John warned the church to evaluate every person who claimed to preach the gospel. Only those who "confess that Jesus Christ has come in the flesh is from God" (1 John 4:2) were true believers. Clearly, the church continued to take this teaching seriously.

Orthodoxy with Diversity

Yet, some scholars disagree with this picture. Seeking a satisfactory explanation of Christianity's early diversity (as seen, for example, in the Petrine, Johannine, and Pauline communities of faith, not to mention the various Gnostic groups), Walter Bauer proposed that some forms of "Christian life" that were later termed heresy were actually the original manifestations of the newly found faith.[18] Various groups throughout the Roman Empire in the first and second centuries expressed forms of Christianity before there was a guiding norm for theology and practice. Therefore, there was nothing like "orthodoxy" or "heresy" in early Christian experience, just different varieties of Christianity. Theologians influenced by this view of Christian history have thus tended to see "orthodoxy" as a misleading label and believed that catholic Christianity only won the day through extreme ecclesiastical and political pressure. A popular example of this thesis is Dan Brown's *Da Vinci Code*, and it is also supported by well-known scholars such as Karen King, Elaine Pagels, and Bart Ehrman. Pagels and King say that the apocryphal Gospel of Judas is "one more retelling of a much-told

18 Walter Bauer, Robert A. Craft, and Gerhard Krodel, *Orthodoxy and Heresy in Earliest Christianity* (Philadelphia: Fortress, 1971), xxii.

tale, but it gives this story a radical new twist, one that turns the tables on 'the twelve.' "[19] Thus, the Gospel of Judas is simply another account of Jesus's life on par with the canonical Gospels. The same could be true for texts such as Gospel of Thomas, the Secret Revelation of John, and the Gospel of Mary, to name a few. According to these scholars, diversity was the order of the day in early Christianity, not uniformity.

And in some ways, they are correct. The witness of early Christianity demonstrates a diversity in culture, worship, and ways of reading Scripture. There was no monolithic church structure as we would see in later centuries but a much more organic, local expression of unity. Such diversity, however, had its theological limits. What had always guided Christians, according to leaders such as Irenaeus, had been the rule of faith. Long after they died, the voices of the apostles continued to reverberate through the active and living word of God as well as the leaders who were ordained to transmit that teaching to the church. There had always been a right way to read Scripture and a wrong way. Thus, Irenaeus gave Christian leaders charged with maintaining truth this clarion call: "This, beloved, is the preaching of the truth, and this is the character of our salvation, and this is the way of life, which the prophets announced and Christ confirmed and the apostles handed over and the Church, in the whole world, hands down to her children."[20]

Lessons for Today

In previous chapters we gleaned wisdom about biblical exegesis from various church fathers, but it is actually Irenaeus who started

19 Elaine Pagels and Karen L. King, *Reading Judas: The Gospel of Judas and the Shaping of Christianity* (New York: Viking, 2007), xv.
20 Irenaeus, *On the Apostolic Preaching*, 298.

it all. From him, we can learn many useful lessons. First, Irenaeus teaches us to read the Bible like the apostles. C. Kavin Rowe argues, "To read the Bible in light of later Trinitarian dogma is to read the Bible in light of the reality of God himself as he has pressured us through his Word, that is, his speaking, to speak about him."[21] We see the beginnings of this habit of reading in the apostles themselves. In his *Apostolic Teaching*, Irenaeus argued that after walking with Christ, learning from him, witnessing his passion and resurrection, and marveling at his ascension, the apostles presented Jesus as the key to all of Scripture. The person and work of Jesus and the indwelling Spirit radically transformed the way they read the Old Testament—as promises fulfilled in the person of Jesus Christ and being fulfilled in the work of the Spirit in the church.

If the Bible is to make sense for life and our world, we need to read like these apostles. When we dissect the Bible beyond recognition, we miss its transformational message and supernatural perspective. The Bible is true regardless of how we atomize it, but its atomic power is harnessed when we present it as one story culminating in the person and work of Christ. We see the beauty and majesty of the triune God and his plan of cosmic redemption when we read the Bible through the apostolic lens. R. B. Jamieson and Tyler Whitman agree that a "deep understanding of Christ leads us to the knowledge of the triune God. Conversely, knowledge of the Trinity is impossible apart from faith in Christ. In order to know one, we must know the other, such that Scripture tends to be theocentric and Christocentric in one breath."[22]

---

21 C. Kavin Rowe, "Biblical Pressure and Trinitarian Hermeneutics," *Pro Ecclesia* 11, no. 3 (2002): 312.

22 R. B. Jamieson and Tyler R. Whitman, *Biblical Reasoning: Christological and Trinitarian Rules for Exegesis* (Grand Rapids, MI: Baker Academic, 2022), 5.

Second, Irenaeus teaches us to see the supernatural world as presented in Scripture. Christians implicitly understand the spiritual nature of reality, yet we often forget that "we do not wrestle against flesh and blood, but against the rulers, against the authorities, against the cosmic powers over this present darkness, against the spiritual forces of evil in the heavenly places" (Eph. 6:12). Irenaeus understood that Gnostic teaching was demonic. This realization activated his pastoral senses, as he knew that those who adhered to false teaching were subject to Satan himself. The Bible reveals that what we see is not always the full picture and that we need a supernatural corrective to our materialistic and decadent modern world. Scripture contains the words of reality, what is true about God, humanity, and the cosmos.

Unfortunately, many have constructed an image of Jesus based on a purely natural view of Christianity wherein faith is based on personal experience and morality measures such faith's validity. Certain religious scholars, like the false religious teachers described by Irenaeus, pick up the jewels and arrange them into a portrait of a fox, claiming it to be a portrayal of the King. Many have purchased this jewel-studded portrait, hung it over their fireplace, and proudly commented on its elegance to their dinner guests. Others hear this portrait described from the pulpits of their churches and in the pages of theology books, not knowing whether this depiction of the biblical God is accurate. Some parade it on talk shows and political rallies as if it is the properly reconstructed likeness of the real thing. Paying little attention to voices such as Irenaeus, they are unable or unwilling to discern whether they have a genuine portrait or a forgery. But pastors following the example of Irenaeus penetrate these false depictions of Jesus with gospel clarity, beckoning people to behold the beauty of the resurrected and reigning Christ.

Last, Irenaeus teaches us how to hold fast to biblical doctrine. We all know this. What we tend to forget, however, is the way that false ideas can subtly permeate our hearts. It begins with a podcast and ends with deconstruction. While we should not be closed-minded people, unable to wrestle with the big ideas of our culture, we should teach in a way that helps Christians discern true ideas from false ones. Believers need to see the beauty in Christian orthodoxy. Trevin Wax notes,

> The ancient Christians worked for decades on arriving at a place of clarity concerning the nature of Christ's identity, not because they were obsessed with the smallest of details or had a propensity toward theological wrangling, but because they knew orthodoxy wasn't some dry, abstract definition—it was a portrait of a real and living God.[23]

Today we live in a world that is built on constant innovation and where only the best innovators survive. Too often pastors burn out because of innovation fatigue. The need to always be creative haunts leaders and churches to the point of despair. This is the plague of our current fascination with authenticity and uniqueness. Following the work of philosopher Charles Taylor, Andrew Root makes this point clear in his book *The Church After Innovation* when he states, "You're authentic when you're uniquely and singularly doing you, when you are living and acting as you wish, creatively presenting your unique self to the world. To be authentic is to be one of a kind."[24] We live in a culture obsessed with being yourself

---

23 Trevin Wax, *The Thrill of Orthodoxy: Rediscovering the Adventure of the Christian Faith* (Downers Grove, IL: Intervarsity, 2022), 43

24 Andrew Root, *The Church After Innovation* (Grand Rapids, MI: Baker Academic, 2022), 15. As Taylor explores in his book *The Ethics of Authenticity*, the idea of authenticity is not new but rather is given new meaning in our culture of hyper-individualism and

and casting off the shackles of what inhibits you from being truly authentic, whatever that may mean. Unfortunately, the church has imbibed much of this unhealthy and dangerous spirit of innovation. But handing over and passing down, as Irenaeus and other early Christian leaders envisioned their task, transcends innovation and reveals the simple yet profound ministry of faithful gospel preaching placed on the shoulders of every gospel minister since the beginning of the church.

Thus the rule of faith used by Irenaeus and the early church is still used by believers today. Truth is always at stake. Whether it's a prosperity gospel that overlooks the sufferings of Christ, a social gospel that minimizes the judgment of Christ, or a liberal gospel that dismisses the miracles of the Bible, Christians are bombarded by false teachings and need to retain a sense of basic gospel principles in order to filter these errors out. When preachers today proclaim a transgender Christ and sexualize his wounds on the cross, the church now, just as before, must maintain a standard of Christian faith that proclaims yes to truth and no to error.[25]

Overall, pastors lead with Scripture. The Bible is their authoritative guide for teaching, preaching, and shepherding. Therefore, to abuse the Bible by twisting it to say and do things it does not is the height of arrogance and pastoral malpractice. Irenaeus and the early church's insistence on the rule of faith does not negate

---

the persistent need to stand out in order to be seen. The concept of authenticity is not unchristian insofar as it means avoiding hypocrisy and embracing one's basic reliance on Christ and our identity in him. When authenticity becomes dangerous is when it assumes that biblical standards for life and doctrine inhibit one's feelings or personal expression regarding issues like sexuality. It can also take on legalistic textures when used to gauge the effectiveness of ministry (by saying a certain church, ministry, or individual is more authentic than another).

25 Jon Brown, "Cambridge Dean Defends Sermon about Jesus' 'Trans Body,' 'Vaginal' Side Wound Blasted as 'Heresy,'" Fox News, November 27, 2022, https://www.foxnews.com/.

pastoral reliance on Scripture—it validates it. He encountered many groups who claimed to have truth but were really in the business of scratching ears to suit their own tastes and passions (2 Tim. 4:3). Thus, for Irenaeus to assert the need for the rule of faith was to affirm what Paul warned Timothy about: "If anyone teaches a different doctrine and does not agree with the sound words of our Lord Jesus Christ and the teaching that accords with godliness, he is puffed up with conceit and understands nothing" (1 Tim. 6:3–4). While Christians may no longer explicitly refer to a rule of faith, we must at all times maintain basic biblical doctrine as the guiding norm for our lives.

Conclusion

In Irenaeus we see a pastor who understood the rich and supernatural realities of the biblical story. Scripture is the oxygen of Christian doctrine and spirituality. Thus, pastors are faithful to their task insofar as they inhabit the world of the Bible for their own souls and the souls of their people. Though the lessons outlined in this chapter are basic, we often lose sight of them during busy seasons of ministry, so it is important to remind ourselves that teaching biblical doctrine cultivates biblical living. As the apostle Paul said to Titus, "hold firm to the trustworthy word as taught, so that [you] may be able to give instruction in sound doctrine and also to rebuke those who contradict it" (Titus 1:9).

6

The Christ-Centered Pastor and Athanasius of Alexandria

We were the purpose of his embodiment, and
for our salvation he so loved human beings as to
come to be and appear in a human body.

ATHANASIUS OF ALEXANDRIA

I decided to know nothing among you except
Jesus Christ and him crucified.

I CORINTHIANS 2:2

EVERY ADVENT, I (COLEMAN) pick up my copy of *On the Incarnation* and do a fresh reading of Athanasius's great work. Though there's no "little Lord Jesus asleep on the hay,"[1] Athanasius conveys the profound mystery of the incarnation of the Son of God and its necessity for the gospel faith. While I love *A Charlie Brown Christmas*, what I need at Christmastime more than a good Vince

---

1   [Martin Luther?], "Away in a Manger," (n.d.).

Guaraldi jazz tune is a sober reminder that a Savior put aside his divine privileges and condescended to take on flesh for the sake of our salvation. Like Linus stepping forward on the school stage to proclaim the true meaning of Christmas from Luke 2, Athanasius stepped forward on the stage of history to proclaim the necessity of the incarnation for our salvation. He stated, "For we were the purpose of his embodiment, and for our salvation he so loved human beings as to come to be and appear in a human body."[2] In his life and ministry, Athanasius fought diligently to emphasize one central truth: no incarnation, no salvation.

Athanasius began his ministry as a deacon assisting his bishop, Alexander, at the Council of Nicaea in 325. After witnessing the proceedings of that initial council, where the theology of Arius of Alexandria was condemned, Athanasius soon became bishop in place of Alexander. His leadership was immediately contested, probably because he was just twenty-nine years old. Yet, he would retain his position for the next forty-six years, punctuated by five separate seasons of exile that totaled seventeen years.

Though Arius was officially denounced at the Council of Nicaea in 325, variations of Arian Christology remained prevalent throughout the church. Disruptions in pneumatology also resulted, forcing Athanasius to respond to critical voices regarding the personhood and divinity of the Spirit. Athanasius exclaimed, "The one who is from God cannot be from nothing, nor can he be a creature—unless they think that the one from whom the Spirit comes is also a creature!"[3] Athanasius was serious about what Scripture said of

2 Saint Athanasius the Great, *On the Incarnation*, trans. John Behr, Popular Patristics Series 44a (Yonkers, NY: St Vladimir's Seminary Press, 2011), 59.

3 Athanasius the Great and Didymus the Blind, *Works on the Spirit*, trans., Mark DelCogliano, Andrew Radde-Gallwitz, and Lewis Ayres, Popular Patristics Series 43 (Yonkers, NY: St Vladimir's Seminary Press, 2011), 87.

the Godhead. Overall, his ministry was marked by the painstaking exegetical, polemical, and pastoral work he did in order to secure the declaration that Christ, as the Nicene Creed states, is "Light from Light" and "true God from true God."[4] Thus, he is a worthy model to follow in considering why pastoral ministry, indeed all of Christian life, is to be Christ-centered.

Defining Christ-Centeredness

Today, the term "Christ-centered" has almost become cliché, being plastered on church websites, Christian living books, and the walls of Christian schools and parachurch ministries. Our (Shawn and Coleman's) pocket of the Christian subculture has cornered the market on being Christ-centered. Yet, though being Christ-centered is an aspect of gospel ministry that must be maintained with every generation, groups that make liberal use of this term are not necessarily living it out. We ourselves recognize that our souls are not as Christ-centered as they should be. We are often too Coleman- or Shawn-centered, career-centered, money-centered, comfort-centered, or coffee-centered. As Elyse Fitzpatrick reminds us,

> Idols aren't just stone statues. . . . They are things that we invest our identity in; they are what we trust. Idols cause us to disregard our heavenly Father in search of what we think we need. Our idols are our loves-gone-wrong: all those things we love more than we love Him, the things we trust for our righteousness or "okay-ness."[5]

4 Shawn J. Wilhite's translation of "The Nicene Creed," sec. 135.c in *Faith in Formulae: A Collection of Early Christian Creeds and Creed-Related Texts*, ed, Wolfram Kinzig, Oxford Early Christian Texts (Oxford: Oxford University Press, 2017), 290.

5 Elyse Fitzpatrick, *Idols of the Heart: Learning to Long for God Alone*, rev. ed, (Phillipsburg, NJ: P&R, 2016), 25–26.

The work of spiritual formation should consistently reorient our hearts to trusting Christ for our righteousness. Our hearts are always prone to wander, and it is the Spirit's work to remind us that Christ is the very source of our life, the only true vine where we abide to remain vibrant and fruitful (John 15). True Christ-centeredness is having Christ as the very core of our identity.

I (Coleman) remember a day in second grade when my parents picked me up after school to travel to the local department store. I had anticipated this day for months—I was going to be an owner of *the* Nintendo Entertainment System (NES), complete with two pads, the Super Mario Bros and Duck Hunt combination cartridge and the orange and grey light gun. I was going to finally experience the glory that was NES gaming. I ate up Mario (though admittedly I was never that good), had fun blasting ducks, and eventually came to enjoy a slew of square grey cartridges. Guides, codes, and helps were created to give players an advantage in games and overcome frustration. One code during this era was infamous: the Konami Code. This code, to be used with many games created by the software company Konami, gave players superpowers and extra lives so that they could become almost invincible. The up-up-down-down-left-right-left-right-B-A-Start maneuver was the difference between life and death in many classic games. Games such as Contra were impossible to beat (at least for subpar players like me), but one simple code unlocked the mystery and allowed me to breeze through to the end (or at least have a better shot).

Just like in Nintendo, we often think our spiritual lives need a Konami Code. If we just had a formula to conquer the Contras of our theology and spirituality, then we would be satisfied. If we could make theological concepts easier to comprehend, then all would be well. Yet, while theology should never be unnecessarily obtuse, it is meant to be deep and vast so as to grasp (as much as humanly possible) the grand mystery of the triune God and his cosmos. It should be explored slowly and carefully with an open Bible and a humble heart. So while we may have creeds and confessions that unpack and explain some of that mystery, there really is no Konami Code for bypassing deep study and reflection empowered and guided by the Holy Spirit. It is this Spirit who helps us commit to Christ-centeredness by continually confessing that it is Christ, not us and our cleverness, who will sustain every molecule of our lives and every desire of our hearts.

Thus, we must maintain at all costs the Christ-centered nature of Christian life and ministry. This spirit is conveyed by the apostle Paul when he said to the Corinthians, "I . . . did not come proclaiming to you the testimony of God with lofty speech or wisdom. For I decided to know nothing among you except Jesus Christ and him crucified" (1 Cor. 2:1–2). Settling for anything less is just trying to cheat ourselves out of the experience, indeed the truthfulness, of the gospel. The person and work of Christ is the true treasure of the Christian. Life explodes with meaning when we find our identity in, rest our hopes on, and continue to learn from Jesus Christ. When the Christ-centered nature of our lives and ministry is disrupted (or even disappears), we become like a ship lost at sea with no light to guide us toward the safe harbors of God's love and mercy. Good Christology is not only necessary for faithful gospel proclamation but also for faithful gospel living. Athanasius and the early church were unanimous on this point: bad doctrine leads to bad living. Going further, the church fathers proclaimed that poor theology began with poor character.[6] This

---

6   In his *De Decretis*, Athanasius remarked, "Therefore, let them prove that their way of thinking is pious. . . . Or, if their conscience is besmirched and they see themselves to be impious,

was not to say that one must have a perfect grasp of the minutiae of theology or be morally perfect to be a faithful Christ follower. Rather, it meant that proper reflection on God and living a godly life was the calling of every Christian. We should want to think deeply, explore the riches of Christ, and pursue holiness with every ounce of our being.

Here is the problem: there are many people and groups who claim to be Christ-centered but are not. How can we make this bold claim? Because some say they are Christ-centered yet have a biblically deficient and theologically poor understanding of Jesus. They may read their Bibles but not with the lens of the apostles, as Irenaeus showed us. What Paul warned Timothy about has happened on repeat throughout church history: "For the time is coming when people will not endure sound teaching, but having itching ears they will accumulate for themselves teachers to suit their own passions, and will turn away from listening to the truth and wander off into myths" (2 Tim. 4:3–4). This is why Paul exhorted Timothy to "preach the word" and "be ready in season and out of season" (2 Tim. 4:2). The "Christ" at the center of some messages is anything but the biblical Jesus. This is where we can learn from Athanasius. In his works, we see that being

---

let them not center what they do not understand, lest they bring upon themselves both the charge of impiety and the reproof of ignorance. Rather, let them enquire into the matter as those who love to learn, so that, coming to know things which they had not known previously, they may cleanse their impious ears with the stream of truth and the doctrines of piety." Khaled Anatolios, trans., *Athanasius* (London: Routledge, 2004), 176, 211. Polemics often led the fathers to make claims regarding the eternal state of heretical teachers, sometimes in ways that seemed presumptuous, because they believed that only those with the indwelling Spirit could reflect properly on Scripture and biblical doctrine. For more on this, particularly as it relates to pneumatological heresies in the fourth century, see Coleman M. Ford, " 'In Your Light We Shall See Light': Virtuous Reading and a Theology of Interpretation in Gregory of Nazianzus's *Oration* 31," *Churchman* 129, vol. 4 (2015): 337–50.

Christ-centered is more than a catchy core value—it affects the entirety of our life and ministry.

Athanasius of Alexandria

It was early in the fourth century that Arius began teaching that the Son was a created being and not coeternal with the Father, saying that there was a time before the Son existed. Bishop Alexander addressed this view and denounced Arius as errant. Not mincing words, Alexander exclaimed of the Arians, "Oh, the impious arrogance! Oh, the immeasurable madness! Oh, the vainglory befitting those that are crazed! Oh, the pride of Satan which has taken root in their unholy souls."[7] Alexander argued that John 1 showed the Son could not be a creature. Though Arius appeared to have some biblical texts to back up his claims, a full reading of Scripture easily refuted his assertions. The Council of Nicaea, which met in 325 under the auspices of Emperor Constantine, formally concluded that the Arian view was heretical and Jesus Christ was "Light from Light, true God from true God."[8] To make this clear, the council adopted the word "homoousias" (from the Greek *homo*, meaning "same," and *ousias*, meaning "being" or "essence") to describe the relationship of the Father and Son. After the council, many church leaders came to believe that this term had modalistic connotations and so the term "homoiousias" (from the Greek *homoi*, meaning "like") was used to replace it.

In his own ministry, Athanasius of Alexandria (296–373) took up the Nicene cause, sparring with various emperors and other

7   James B. H. Hawkins, "Alexander of Alexandria: Translator's Introductory Notice," in *Fathers of the Third Century: Gregory Thaumaturgus, Dionysius the Great, Julius Africanus, Anatolius and Minor Writers, Methodius, Arnobius*, ed. Alexander Roberts, James Donaldson, and A. Cleveland Coxe (Buffalo, NY: Christian Literature Company, 1886), 6:295.

8   "The Nicene Creed."

church leaders throughout the fourth century, many of whom were either Arian in conviction (e.g., Constantius, Valens) or pagan in disposition (e.g., Julian). Through works such as his *Four Discourses against Arians*, *On the Incarnation*, and *Letters*, Athanasius defended an orthodox view of the Trinity and provided a theological foundation for others to follow. For Athanasius and those after him, Nicaea was more than winning a theological battle of words—the souls of humanity hung in the balance. Disturbing the biblical tension of the person and work of Christ could lead to detrimental and eternal spiritual consequences.

Combatting False Christology

Athanasius sought to combat such errors in his *Four Discourses against the Arians*. These discourses demonstrate a full exegetical and polemical assault on Arian theology. Athanasius systematically addressed every "problem" text that appeared to relegate the person of Christ to the status of creature rather than Creator and argued that the Arians' so-called "private sense" of (i.e., special insight into) reading Scripture only led to misinterpretation and grave error.[9] For example, to refute the Arian interpretation of Hebrews 1, Athanasius asserted,

> Regarding the Word's visitation in the flesh, and the Economy which He then sustained, [the writer of Hebrews] wished to shew that He was not like those who had gone before Him; so that, as much as He excelled in nature those who were sent afore by

9 Athanasius of Alexandria, "Four Discourses against the Arians," in *St. Athanasius: Select Works and Letters*, ed. Philip Schaff and Henry Wace, trans. John Henry Newman and Archibald T. Robertson, vol. 4, *A Select Library of the Nicene and Post-Nicene Fathers of the Christian Church, Second Series* (New York: Christian Literature Company, 1892), 327–28.

Him, by so much also the grace which came from and through Him was better than the ministry through Angels.[10]

In other words, comparison language in Scripture does not intend to speak about Christ's divine nature—this is where Arians, and any who challenge the divinity of Christ, went horribly awry. Read in isolation, any biblical text could mean whatever you want it to. But Scripture does not contradict itself and thus must be read as a cohesive unit. Christians do not choose which portions of Scripture to agree with; rather, they receive the whole.

Promoting True Christology

Athanasius demonstrated this cohesive reading of Scripture in his classic work of Christian theology, *On the Incarnation*. The detrimental consequences of misreading the biblical witness are made even more explicit in this text. Here, Athanasius argued that the incarnation of Christ is a necessary piece of information for the doctrine of salvation. Though Christians do not need to have a full theological understanding of the incarnation in order to be saved, misguided teaching can lead people to believe a different gospel and thus hinder the proclamation of the true gospel.

Overall, Athanasius framed the necessity of Christ's incarnation within the reality of humanity's fall and corruption. As the pinnacle of creation, God did not want humanity to remain in sin. Athanasius explained that it "was supremely improper that the workmanship of God in human beings should disappear either through their own negligence or through the deceit of the demons."[11] Thus, this good God reached out in love to save his creation by sending his

10 Athanasius, "Four Discourses," bk. 1, chap. 11, sec. 37.
11 Athanasius, *On the Incarnation*, 6.

Son. Though this incarnation was a specific moment in redemption history, the Word is eternally existing and present in all places. Therefore, humanity has never been without the Word, though at a specific point "the Word became flesh and dwelt among us" (John 1:14) to inaugurate the next phase of human redemption. This Word upholds all of creation but also has a unique relationship with humanity. Theologian Khaled Anatolios explains,

> Whereas all other creatures participate in the Word's power in the strictly passive mode of being "governed" by the Word, humanity's participation is in the mode of a conscious sharing in the active "rationality" of the Word; among all creatures, only humanity possesses the "greater grace" of being *logikos*. As such, humanity actively and intentionally shares in the power of the Logos and rejoices in this participation.[12]

In other words, because human beings are rational, being created by a rational God, the incarnation was necessary to unite rational humanity to rational Word. To heal their corruption, God needed to apply the incorruptibility of his divine nature. He thus took upon himself the nature of humanity to introduce humanity to the nature of God. Athanasius insisted that as "human beings had turned towards corruption [Christ] might turn them again to incorruptibility and give them life from death, by making the body his own and by the grace of the resurrection banishing death from them as straw from the fire."[13] Christ performed this act out of love for humanity.

Thus, to proclaim the person and work of Christ, according to the testimony of Athanasius, is to simultaneously declare the love

---

12 Anatolios, *Athanasius*, 34.
13 Athanasius, *On the Incarnation*, 8.

of God for his creation. It seems then that there is something innate in humanity that prompted God to act for their benefit. The simple fact that they are made in his image, being a good creation from a good God, made the incarnation a necessity. John 3:16 is a profound declaration of this truth: "For God so loved the world that he gave his only Son, that whoever believes in him should not perish but have eternal life." In return, this divine love represented in the incarnation ought to lead Christians toward love of God and others.

A Christ-Centered Spirituality

Another one of Athanasius's texts, *Life of Antony*, shows us this kind of loving Christian life. The region of Alexandria, Egypt, where Athanasius ministered was a hub of Christian spiritual and intellectual activity. It was there that ascetic Christians retreated to the desert, and Athanasius, being close by, greatly affected them. Some of them were influenced by him too, like the monk Antony, who was a vocal supporter of Athanasius. Antony was renowned for his austerity and soon after his death, many Christians desired to know more about him. Athanasius responded to these numerous appeals by writing his famous biography, which became his most influential work. This work was a bestseller in his own time, being read by countless believers, including the likes of Augustine of Hippo. For these readers, Antony's life story personalized the gospel's call of obedience to Christ and his commands. Robert Gregg notes that the "career of Antony . . . confronted the Church and its members with a radical definition of Christian identity and purpose."[14] It is no surprise that Antony was such a popular

---

14 Robert C. Gregg, "Introduction," in *Athanasius: The Life of Antony and the Letter to Marcellinus*, ed. Richard J. Payne, trans. Robert C. Gregg, The Classics of Western Spirituality (Mahwah, NJ: Paulist Press, 1980), 6.

figure in the early to mid-fourth century, as this was an age of massive spiritual transition. Emperor Constantine gave the church imperial legitimacy, most emperors who followed continued to identify with Christianity in some way, and the church became more visible than it had ever been before. This had positive effects, such as a decrease in persecution, but it also had negative effects—with notoriety came the temptation toward spiritual lethargy. Identifying as a Christian was no longer dangerous but desired. With the likelihood of physical martyrdom all but extinguished, spiritual martyrs became the prime example of Christian faith and practice. Hence, for those looking for serious spiritual mentors, Antony was a hero.

Though reared in a Christian household, Antony's spiritual journey only began in earnest after the death of his parents. During a season of reflecting on the self-sacrifice of those early Christ followers, Antony responded to the reading of Matthew 19:21 in a worship service by selling all his possessions and living a life of total dedication to God. His life from that point on was marked by paying serious attention to the Scripture and the commands of God. This included frequent prayer (inspired by 1 Thess. 5:17), working to sustain his basic needs (inspired by 2 Thess. 3:10), and memorizing Scriptures. His piety earned him the nickname "God-loved."[15] His attention to holy living invited the temptation of Satan, but he bravely met this with increased dedication to the Lord. Athanasius recounted, "In thinking about the Christ and considering the excellence won through him, and the intellectual part of the soul, Antony extinguished the fire of his opponent's deception."[16]

---

15 Richard J. Payne, ed., *Athanasius: The Life of Antony and the Letter to Marcellinus*, The Classics of Western Spirituality (Mahwah, NJ: Paulist Press, 1980), 4.

16 Payne, *Life of Antony*, 5.

Athanasius went on to describe the austerity of Antony as seen in his habits of dress, sleep, and fasting. Such practices stemmed from a desire for purification from the pleasures and lusts of this world. His pursuit of ascetic living was mostly done in solitude, though he persuaded many others to pursue a similar life and shared his wisdom with others, careful to extol the Scriptures as the final rule of faith and practice. He once exhorted several Christian brothers by saying,

> Let none among us have even the yearning to possess. For what benefit is there in possessing these things that we do not take with us? Why not rather own those things that we are able to take away with us—such things as prudence, justice, temperance, courage, understanding, love, concern for the poor, faith in Christ, freedom from anger, hospitality? If we possess these, we shall discover them running before, preparing hospitality for us there in the land of the meek.[17]

Such wisdom did not come through the knowledge of worldly philosophy but God's word. After an exchange with some philosophers, Antony stated, "We Christians, then, do not possess the mystery in a wisdom of Greek reasonings, but in the power supplied to us by God through Jesus Christ."[18] While there is much to be learned in the world, true wisdom is only found with God.

Yet, this kind of Christian living brings with it opposition from Satan. To encourage those who experienced such warfare, Antony asserted, "We need, therefore, to fear God alone, holding [demons] in contempt and fearing them not at all. Indeed, the more they

17 Payne, *Life of Antony*, 17.
18 Payne, *Life of Antony*, 78.

do these things, let us all the more exert ourselves in the discipline that opposes them, for a great weapon against them is a just life and trust in God."[19] Those who have placed their hope and trust in Christ can always look to him in times of trial and despair.

In sum, Athanasius depicted Antony as a Christian warrior living contrary to the hopes and expectations of the world who encourages believers to remain diligent in our practice of holy living. Like Paul, they are to die daily to themselves (1 Cor. 15:31). They are to set their minds on "whatever is true, whatever is honorable, whatever is just, whatever is pure, whatever is lovely, whatever is commendable" (Phil. 4:8). This is not a onetime decision but an hour-by-hour, day-by-day pursuit of the things of God. Empowered by the Spirit, Christians must make the daily decision to own their spiritual growth and pursue godly living.

Lessons for Today

Athanasius's works teach us much about this godly living, but three lessons that stand out are the importance of staying faithful to the great tradition, the beauty of simple living, and the reality of the spiritual realm. First, Athanasius reminds us that biblical interpretation does not take place in a vacuum but relies on the work of Christians in previous eras. There are many practical ways we can follow in his footsteps. Considering and reflecting on the creedal formulations of the early councils is a good place to start. This does not mean we must slavishly follow tradition or every interpretive rabbit trail taken throughout church history. We should follow, however, the time-tested and well-worn path of biblical interpretation built on Christ and the apostolic message. We see this from

19 Payne, *Life of Antony*, 30.

Irenaeus discussed earlier, but Athanasius gives us additional perspective on biblical interpretation when he warns readers to avoid what the Arians called a "private sense" of Scripture.

Protestants, especially evangelical Protestants, are often chided by older high church traditions for practicing a private sense of interpretation. However, in reality, the foundation of biblical interpretation built during the Reformation does not allow for that.[20] In fact, interpretive errors were exactly what the Reformers were seeking to correct. They believed that biblical interpretation had been corrupted by the hermeneutical blueprint of the Roman Catholic Church. Using that method, the Bible was not seen as the clear story of God's redemptive work but was clouded by centuries of conciliar decisions and papal decrees. Though the Reformers were accused of private interpretation by the Roman Catholic Church because they were out of step with its doctrine, they rebutted by asserting that the Roman Church was out of step with Scripture itself and the first centuries of Christian thinkers. Overall, the Reformers never promoted private interpretation but rather a return to the primacy of Scripture as its own interpreter with the aid of early voices like Athanasius who understood the same principle.

Thus, to be faithful Protestants, we must read and interpret the Scriptures in light of Scripture, adhering to the biblically warranted formulas of Christian orthodoxy forged in the early centuries of the church. Reading Scripture with the fathers is a practice that brings more, not less, clarity to the biblical text. Further, to be faithful Protestants we must not assert that all readers are authorized to

---

20 For more information on the biblical interpretation and reading habits of the Reformers see Timothy George, *Reading Scripture with the Reformers* (Downers Grove, IL: IVP Academic, 2011).

interpret the Bible as they see fit. We read the Bible first by listening for the echoes of some parts of Scripture in other parts of Scripture. Scripture interprets Scripture, and in the places where we have less clarity, we speak cautiously and always point to the grander story of Scripture and the authority of the text in all matters.

Second, Athanasius's account of Antony's life shows us the beauty of simple living and the reality of the spiritual realm. Though our culture and context look much different from the fourth-century Roman Empire, we have similar spiritual issues. Like Christianity in the fourth century, many of us live with the assumption that our society is Christianized, and some even advocate for even further Christianization. While none of us should lament when the gospel takes hold of people and cultures, we need to remember the danger that always lurks around the corner: spiritual laziness. We live in a culture that strives for ease. Every advertisement on your social media feed promises to make your life easier in some way and many innovations have allowed us to complete tasks in seconds that once took months or years. Of course, it is not wrong to have a more efficient and less stressful life. But with such innovation, our capacity for patience and hard work has regressed. In our search for ease, we are more annoyed at the lack of instant results. Thus, a life of austerity and dedication to the time-tested disciplines of godliness fly in the face of our culture of convenience. The example of Antony reminds us that pursuing Christlikeness is never easy but always rewarding.

While we do not advocate that everyone should sell all they have as Antony and many early monks did (from their under-standing of Matt. 19:16–29), materialism plagues the Western church. Sometimes it matters more what car we drive and what gym we belong to than the vitality of our church fellowship and our growth in self-denial. It is possible that purses and politics define Western Christians more than the pursuit of holiness. What we learn from Antony is that not only will God meet our needs but he will also carry us through the numerous trials of life, and someone who pursues God away from all comforts to feed the soul with biblical wisdom cannot help but have God's wisdom pour forth from them.

When you strip away the façade that materialism creates and drink deeply from God's wisdom in his word, you also begin to see reality more clearly, and that reality shows a spiritual war being fought all around us. Being surrounded by naturalism, Christian spirituality in the West would do well to have a fresh injection of understanding the reality of spiritual warfare. Scripture does not allow us to view our lives apart from spiritual realities. While this does not mean every cancer diagnosis or lost cell phone has a demon behind it, it does mean that our experience is inescapably marked by spiritual battle. It may not be a pastor's job to exorcise demons, but it is the job of the pastor (and any mature Christian) to help others walk through spiritual battles in reliance on God's word and his Spirit. Spiritual warfare only intensifies after coming to Christ and seeking to walk faithfully in step with his Spirit. Thus, the more we wish to honor the Lord, the more we will probably encounter opposition. Antony's life demonstrates this reality with full focus and intensity. Emphasizing a simple trust in God, he knew that looking to God rather than focusing on our struggles and trials was the remedy for any spiritual ailment.

When I (Coleman) began trumpet lessons, the first thing I had to learn was how to blow properly into the mouthpiece. The shiny brass trumpet sat in its case for the first few weeks as I figured out proper lip placement. But eventually the mouthpiece had to be inserted in the trumpet. No one learns to play the trumpet just for the mouthpiece—the trumpet itself must be played in order to produce the bright and vibrant sounds. Whether you want to play a concerto from Haydn or a Miles Davis solo, learning the mouthpiece is the first step, but it is not the last. This is like the Christian life. Union with Christ is the vital first step, and indeed nothing else in our Christian life can be played without it. This union, however, is meant to bring out vibrant spiritual melodies seen in our thoughts, words, and actions. This is what Antony's life shows us. The empowerment of God must lead to diligent work to produce a beautiful Christian life. After rereading the *Life of Antony*, I was struck with Antony's vigor for the Christian life. This is no spirituality for the weak. Antony is depicted as a spiritual warrior but not as one who musters spiritual strength on his own—his strength comes from the Holy Spirit. And, therefore, his spirituality is modeled on the life of Christ.

Conclusion

In *On the Incarnation*, Athanasius helps readers understand the dire spiritual consequences of neglecting the incarnation of Christ and points readers toward Christ-focused living. The Christian hope is not found in the latest church program but in the eternal person of Christ. All Christian ministry is fueled and sustained by the preaching, teaching, and spirituality of Christ in his full person and work. Thus, until we accept what that it is not us but Christ in us that brings life-transformation through ministry work (Gal. 2:20–21), we will inevitably hit a wall. So instead of chasing the latest fad for our ministry, we should seek the firmest foundation for our ministry—the person and work of Jesus Christ. Basing our teaching, preaching, and discipleship on the biblical and orthodox doctrine of Christ will always produce fruit and never return empty (Isa. 55:11; John 15:4–5).

This is exactly what is seen in Athanasius's *Life of Antony*. Austerity is often praised but rarely practiced. Antony shows us that simple living—rejecting obsession with material possessions and redirecting one's energy to learning God's wisdom—is worth it. Hundreds of years ago, he confronted the lethargic Christian world with the challenge of his austere spiritual life. Believers like this can confront the Christian world yet again.

7

The Theological Pastor and Augustine of Hippo

One only loves, after all, what delights one.

AUGUSTINE OF HIPPO

You shall love the Lord your God with all your heart
and with all your soul and with all your mind.
This is the great and first commandment.

MATTHEW 22:37–38

MANY PASTORS DESIRE to continue learning after seminary. I (Shawn) once decided to explore one scholarly issue in a different field (e.g., New Testament studies, church history, Greek) per month for a year. As you can imagine, my appetite for theological and ministerial development was far too large for my pastoral schedule. I only finished one or two books before work duties began to pile up and I threw my original plan out the window. Now, years later, my schedule remains full, but I have learned how to make time for reading. I knew I would flounder as a thinker, pastor, and burgeoning scholar if I did not make some serious changes. So, rather than allowing other people to run my schedule, I took control of my own life to make space for all the good things I knew I should be doing—work, spiritual disciplines, and quality time with my family.

For the pastor, busyness is a disease that eventually erodes time for reflection and makes him nothing more than a facilitator of meetings. But the church needs ministers who have wrestled with philosophical and theological issues. Only then can they truly help parishioners understand the deeper things of God and bring out the riches of Christian theology for the joy of their congregants. Every pastor is a theologian, and the more we lean into that reality, the more spiritually mature our people will become.

Theology Begins and Ends with God

As we've already seen, theology is first and foremost for the benefit of the church. But what precisely is theology? It is the study of God, the main ontological reality, as revealed to us in his creation and word. All other subsets of theology are derivatives of the study of God himself. Thus, John Webster says, "We need to ask what Scripture and reason *are* and what they are *for*."[1] In other words, we must maintain a robust philosophical ontology of Scripture and a spiritually meaningful teleology of theology.

In sum, we must remember that Scripture is from (and thus subordinate to) God and exists for the purpose of revealing God. This may seem obvious but many of us (perhaps subconsciously) can accidentally commit a subtle kind of bibliolatry that situates

---

1   John Webster, *The Domain of the Word: Scripture and Theological Reason*, T&T Clark Theology (London: Bloomsbury, 2012), 115.

Scripture as the main ontological reality. We need to remember that it is God who is the main ontological reality and that he exists with (or hypothetically without) the Scriptures. The Scriptures fit within the economy (i.e., external work) of God, who reveals himself and relates to creation. If God is the prime reality, all things that exist come from him (including Scripture). This means that in our theological study, belief in God must precede all else. As Augustine asserted, "Do not try to understand in order to believe, but believe in order to understand."[2]

Webster sums all of this up for us when he says,

> The Holy Trinity is the ontological principle (*principium essendi*) of Christian theology; its external or objective cognitive principle (*principium cognoscendi externum*) is the Word of God presented through the embassy of the prophets and apostles; its internal or subject cognitive principle (*principium cognoscendi internum*) is the redeemed intelligence of the saints.[3]

Thus, we hold up our Bibles not for the Bible's sake but as a way to see God (as we also do in creation and the incarnation).

With greater clarity on ontology, the telos of theology can then be determined. In short, the purpose of theology is to gain greater communion with God and his creation. This applies to the pastor, as we have explained in chapter 2, but also spills over from his life into the life of the church. Using Psalm 85:8, Webster masterfully speaks about the role of theology and the life of the church when

---

2 Saint Augustine, *Homilies on the Gospel of John 1–40*, ed. Allan D. Fitzgerald and Boniface Ramsey, trans. Edmund Hill, vol. 12, The Works of Saint Augustine: A Translation for the 21st Century (Hyde Park, NY: New City, 2009), 493.

3 Webster, *Domain of the Word*, 135.

he says, "Let me hear what God the Lord will speak, for he will speak peace to his people, to his saints, to those who turn to him in their hearts."[4] Webster further explains this at length, and it will be helpful to see three parts of his explanation side by side:

> Theology is an aspect of the church's intelligent participation in the order of peace. . . . Theology is both contemplative and apostolic. Contemplative first, because whatever it may offer to the church derives from sustained and disciplined and unselfish attention to divine revelation in its limitless depth and scope; everything depends upon contemplative absorption in God and the gospel of peace. Apostolic second and by derivation, because the rule of charity in the church requires that gifts be communicated, not hoarded, such that theology is part of the flow of love.[5]

> Theology, then, serves the church in its imperfect state by attending to and speaking about, the God of peace and the peace of God. The intellectual work of attention and speech constitutes the enduring vocation of theology (other critical and historical responsibilities are occasional and subordinate).[6]

> Theology shares the imperfection of all the saints. In advance of our beatification, theology is ectypal, only the faintest reproduction of God's self-knowledge, revealed, not native, preserved by labour, devoid of comprehensiveness. And theology is entangled with sin at every point. . . . Theology in the condition of pilgrims

4 Webster, *Domain of the Word*, 150–51.
5 Webster, *Domain of the Word*, 164.
6 Webster, *Domain of the Word*, 164.

is not a transcendent moment, a point of pure perception or participation in the divine wisdom; it is a work of reason in the domain where reconciliation has not yet been perfectly appropriated or reached its creaturely term.[7]

As pilgrims, we are working through our experience with God. We participate imperfectly in the life of God, yet theology does not stifle spirituality. It is not archaic, reserved only for scholars with tweed jackets and disheveled hair. Theology is for the Christian who suffers from cancer and the Christian who is afflicted with anxiety and depression. Theology is for a happy life of loving God and others, for Christians and the church to reflect on God and be transformed by his presence.

Augustine of Hippo

Augustine of Hippo (354–430) provides an excellent model of what it looks like in real life to be a theological pastor. His life and thought, well known to many through his *Confessions*, *On Christian Doctrine*, *On the Trinity*, *City of God*, and other works, help us better understand how to commit ourselves to the goal of theology: to know and love God.

It is not an exaggeration to say that Augustine directed the course of theology for the next 1500 years after him. Indeed, even during his life, his voice was often seen as definitive on matters of doctrine. From the nature of grace to ecclesiology, the Trinity, and more, Augustine contributed greatly to the field of theology. But, like many figures we have discussed thus far, Augustine was primarily a pastor. Though often portrayed as a controversialist, his theology

7   Webster, *Domain of the Word*, 165.

was frequently developed and expressed in his preaching, with the lives of his friends and church in mind. Thus, with Augustine as their guide, pastors today can learn how to devote themselves to God by doing theology, form a robust interior life with God as their constant companion, seek out mentors to help them develop deeper theological awareness, respond effectively to their people's theological concerns, and cultivate friendships for spiritual growth.

Loving God by Doing Theology

Augustine challenges pastors today when he says, "Anyone who thinks that he has understood the divine scriptures or any part of them, but cannot by his understanding build up this double love of God and neighbor, has not yet succeeded in understanding them."[8] Augustine understood that to fulfill our calling as leaders, we need to fulfill our duty to love God and others. This simple yet profound command is the trellis on which every ministry vine grows, and it is made up of both acts of service and contemplation of God. Though it may not seem so on the surface, the latter is also an act of love. Jesus said, "You shall love the Lord your God with all your heart and with all your soul and *with all your mind*" (Matt. 22:37). Thus, contemplative theology nourishes our love for God. When we engage in theological reflection, whether reading a book on theological anthropology or a journal article on inseparable operations, we are being faithful to the call to love God.

Not everyone is a profound theological thinker, but you do not need to be one to be faithful to loving God with your mind. All you need to do is grow in your theological depth more regularly and consistently. This does not mean that pastors need to know

8   Augustine, *Saint Augustine: On Christian Teaching*, trans. R. P. H. Green, Oxford World's Classics (Oxford: Oxford University Press, 1997), bk. 1, secs. 84–96.

everything but that they put in the necessary time to train their minds for the sake of properly administering spiritual care to the best of their ability. Consider the medical field. Would you want to undergo surgery with a doctor who has not learned anything new since med school? What would such lack of interest in new procedures and insights say about this doctor? At best, they are lazy. At worst, they are negligent and possibly liable to harm. The same can be said of pastors, so we should expect them to seek continuing education as well. Even more than others, they should desire to keep learning because their teacher is none other than the triune God of the universe.

The Interior Life

Every spring, I (Coleman) sit down with students in my Great Books of Late Antiquity class and get excited that we will eventually read Augustine's *Confessions*. Not a year has gone by in over a decade that I haven't studied this book, and I usually try to read a different translation each time. In this class we also read Roman authors such as Virgil, Plutarch, and Marcus Aurelius. Epic poetry, moral biography, and Stoic wisdom are all part of the Roman literary tradition and are important for us to read. None of these, however, convey the richness of the interior life of the soul as well as Augustine. In fact, this is not how typical Romans conceived of religion at all. Religion was public and familial, with moves and gestures intended to demonstrate piety toward family and state.[9] Thus, Virgil's *Aeneid* became the identity-shaping epic for Roman people because Aeneas demonstrated loyalty to family and honored

---

9 For more information on piety in ancient Rome, see William Chase Greene and John Scheid, "Pietas" in *The Oxford Classical Dictionary*, eds. Simon Hornblower, Antony Spawforth, and Esther Eidinow, 4th ed. (Oxford: Oxford University Press, 2012).

the gods. Never once did Aeneas consider how his soul longed for a relationship with Zeus, and he was not concerned that his lustful encounter with Dido meant something was faulty in his heart. Greeks and Romans had no conception of connecting intimately to the divine, and those who claimed to do so were seen with great suspicion. So when Christians came on the scene, their claims of a personal relationship with God through Christ seemed bizarre. Augustine would become the first to show how this deep inner dialogue was pivotal to one's spiritual vitality.

The idea of the inward turn to the soul was first seen in the Neoplatonists, mainly Plotinus (ca. 204–270), but took biblical and theological shape with Augustine. Neoplatonists discerned a link between the soul and the Good; Augustine gave theological vocabulary to this link.[10] In fact, his *Confessions* is one long prayer beginning with a reflection on mortality and the greatness of God. He searched the depths of his soul to understand both his longing for happiness as well as its fulfillment in knowing God.

We have previously discussed this concept, especially in chapter 2, but what is unique in Augustine is the way his inner life contributed to his theological reasoning. Observing this aspect of Augustine's thought, Josh Chatraw and Mark Allen note, "Before Augustine composed *The City of God*, with its penetrating societal critique and apologetically aimed redemptive narrative, he first journeyed into his own soul—critiquing his own idolatries and learning to map the story of grace onto his own life. In short, *Confessions* led him to *The City*."[11] The same can be said for his *On the Trinity*, which

10 For more on the Platonist tradition of interiority and Augustine's theological appropriation of it see Philip Cary, *Augustine's Invention of the Inner Self: The Legacy of a Christian Platonist* (Oxford: Oxford University Press, 2000).
11 Joshua D. Chatraw and Mark D. Allen, *The Augustine Way: Retrieving a Vision for the Church's Apologetic Witness* (Grand Rapids, MI: Baker Academic, 2023), 104.

demonstrates deep interior reflection, as well as his anti-Pelagian books, which work from the premise of humanity's need for God's grace in salvation and faithful perseverance in the Christian life.

It is tempting to view the *Confessions* as two unrelated units. Books 1 through 9 recount the story of Augustine's spiritual journey, while books 10 through 13 read more like lofty speculation and esoteric ponderings as Augustine converses with God on the nature of memory, time, and creation. Some of us might therefore want to stop reading *Confessions* after book 9, but to fully understand Augustine, we must persevere through the end. Augustine, through inner dialogue with God, considered both the sovereign grace of God in his salvation as well as the sovereign grace of God in his creation. Both spheres of theological reflection are necessary in order to grow in one's wonder and dependence upon the God of the universe. Seeing grace in salvation leads to seeing grace throughout all of life.

There is not one corner of the cosmos where Augustine did not perceive God's grace at work. At the end of book 11, Augustine declared, "Lord my God, how deep is your profound mystery, and how far away from it have I been thrust by the consequences of my sins. Heal my eyes and let me rejoice with your light."[12] After pages of theological reflection, Augustine continued to confess his need for healing in light of God's greatness and mystery.

This shows us that the way to cultivate an interior life with God for the sake of knowing him is through repentance and rejoicing. Even though we carry around with us a reminder of our own sin and mortality, we have a longing in our anxious hearts that is only satisfied in God.[13] When we enter the office on Monday morning,

---

12 Augustine, *Confessions*, trans. Henry Chadwick, Oxford World's Classics (Oxford: Oxford University Press, 1998), 11.31.41.
13 Augustine, *Confessions* 1.1.1.

we enter into an opportunity to sit and commune with the Lord as part of our vocation. Learning theology is first generating and cultivating an intimate conversation with God, and part of cultivating the inner dialogue with God is growing in our gratitude for his grace, which has the effect of transforming our doxology and reinforcing our orthodoxy. In moments of bitterness, anxiety, and stress, our lack of gratitude for God's work is often a major factor. This does not mean that every emotional and psychological problem is solved by being more thankful, but it does mean that much of the ministry stress we feel stems from forgetting the sovereign grace of God and his specific work of grace in our own lives. Cultivating the inner life through prayer leads to gratitude, which then lays the foundation for theological study and ministry praxis.

Theological Mentors

Augustine shows us that our theology and ministry can also benefit from mentorship. Toward the beginning of his work on the Trinity, he notes his indebtedness to prior commentators:

> The purpose of all the Catholic commentators I have been able to read on the divine books of both testaments, who have written before me on the trinity which God is, has been to teach that according to the scriptures Father and Son and Holy Spirit in the inseparable equality of one substance present a divine unity.[14]

Here, we see Augustine's desire to be mentored, even by those who came centuries before him, in the content of theology and in the task of doing theology.

14 Saint Augustine, *The Trinity (De Trinitate)*, ed. John E. Rotelle, 2nd ed, The Works of Saint Augustine: A Translation for the 21st Century (Hyde Park, NY: New City, 2017), 1:70.

One of the foremost mentors in Augustine's life was Ambrose of Milan, whose preaching he listened to before his conversion. We have already discussed the sacramental nature of ministry according to Ambrose, but what we did not mention was the profound effect his preaching had on the surrounding community. Craig Satterlee notes that Ambrose was persuasive and influential not just because of his position as bishop but because he was a "talented speaker and trained rhetorician with new insight into the Scripture."[15] It was this new insight into Scripture that drew Augustine in. After first arriving in Milan and hearing Ambrose, Augustine said, "More and more my conviction grew that all the knotty problems and clever calumnies which those deceivers of ours had devised against the divine books could be dissolved."[16] In Ambrose's preaching, the mysteries of God's word were unlocked, and Augustine began to see the beauty of the biblical narrative unfold before him. Augustine would go on to be baptized by Ambrose in 387 and continued to see him as a theological mentor for the remainder of his life, using the affectionate language of "our Ambrose" in his writings.[17] He conferred with Ambrose while he was still living and read the works of Ambrose throughout the remainder of his ministry. It was clear that the life and theology of Ambrose had a significant impact on the thought of Augustine, situating him squarely within the Nicene tradition.

Augustine also pursued mentorship and theological camaraderie with others he encountered. Though many considered him

---

15 Craig Alan Satterlee, *Ambrose of Milan's Method of Mystagogical Preaching* (Collegeville, MN: Liturgical, 2002), 108.

16 Augustine, *Confessions* 6.3.4.

17 See Augustine, *Epistles* 75, 82, 147, 148 in *Saint Augustine: Letters*, ed. Sister Wilfrid Parsons, Fathers of the Church 12 (Washington, DC: The Catholic University of America Press, 1951), vols. 1 and 3.

a mentor, Augustine sought counsel and advice from peers and older clergy alike.[18] He exchanged letters with Jerome (which were a bit heated at times)[19] and served as a spiritual guide and friend to Paulinus of Nola and Alypius in order to foster mutual growth in Christlikeness. Thus, Augustine was both a mentor in virtue as well as a student of it.

Awareness of Your People

I (Coleman) remember when I was a young minister and fresh seminary student. I was excited about the training I was receiving and my pastoral work. Learning theology, church history, and hermeneutics was more than theoretical—it was all directly applied to my ministry each week. Early on as a youth minister, I decided to do a Bible study with students on the book of Mark, intending to employ the exegetical and hermeneutical principles I was learning in school. It was going well (or so I thought) until one week I realized that I was simply lecturing about the intricacies of the biblical text rather than discussing its practical benefits. I was more concerned about showing off my newly acquired skills than addressing how the Bible spoke to the lives and challenges of these students. I see this often in the seminary and ministry contexts where I serve, and I understand the zeal of young ministers because that was me many years ago. What we need, however, is to use such newly acquired skills to address the actual heart issues of the people we serve. Theology should not be purely contextual, only existing to address the desires and needs of church members.

18 For more on the mentoring aspect of Augustine's ministry see Edward L. Smither, *Augustine as Mentor: A Model for Preparing Spiritual Leaders* (Nashville: B&H Academic, 2009).

19 For more on the relationship between Augustine and Jerome as a form of corrective love see Coleman M. Ford, *A Bond between Souls: Friendship in the Letters of Augustine* (Bellingham, WA: Lexham, 2022), chap. 3.

But it is always contextualized, applying the timeless truth of God's word to the timely situations of God's people.

Augustine understood this concept well. We see this in how he addressed his listeners when preaching. For example, on the anniversary of Augustine's ordination, likely toward the end of his life, he preached about the need for his listeners to live good lives and his own desire to not be unduly praised by them. He confessed, "Now my danger is this: if I pay attention to how you praise me and take no notice of the sort of lives you lead."[20] Though we may lack detail into how Augustine particularly approached specific people in his congregation, we see here a deep sense of concern for the spiritual and moral lives of those under his care. His "burden" was to see them remain faithful and continue growing, just as the apostle Peter encouraged the church to grow in the "grace and knowledge of our Lord and Savior Jesus Christ" (2 Pet. 3:18).

In another sermon given on the anniversary of his ordination, Augustine showed a similar concern and expanded on the pastoral care necessary for different groups of people. He preached,

> The turbulent have to be corrected, the faint-hearted cheered up, the weak supported; the gospel's opponents need to be refuted, its insidious enemies guarded against; the unlearned need to be taught, the indolent stirred up, the argumentative checked; the proud must be put in their place, the desperate set on their feet, those engaged in quarrels reconciled; the needy have to be helped, the oppressed to be liberated, the good to be given

20 Saint Augustine, *Sermons 306–340A on the Saints*, ed. John E. Rotelle, trans. Edmund Hill, The Works of Saint Augustine: A Translation for the 21st Century (Hyde Park, NY: New City, 1994), 9:279.

your backing, the bad to be tolerated; all must be loved. In all the vast and varied activity involved in fulfilling such manifold responsibilities, please give me your help by both your prayers and your obedience. In this way I will find pleasure not so much in being in charge of you as in being of use to you.[21]

Thus, Augustine did not view the pastorate as an opportunity to gain power over people, fulfill personal vanity, or a platform on which to build his own brand. Rather, the pastorate was an opportunity to walk with and minister to others, addressing their needs and speaking to the concerns of their life. He wanted to be of use to the church, and his writings from the shortest letter to his massive *City of God* were in service to people he loved and wished to see formed in the gospel.

How many pastors have the sense of being "of use" to their people in terms of their theological reflection and output? To be of use is to set about the task of knowing our people and responding with the proper biblical and theological remedies to address their spiritual ailments. Being of use does not mean being used in a pejorative sense but humbly offering yourself to your people as a vessel of God's grace and mercy to them. It includes things like addressing the idols of our culture in the pulpit, reminding couples in marriage counseling of their union with Christ, developing classes in apologetics, theology, and church history to inform and train our people in the faith, and cultivating church members' spiritual gifts for the good of the kingdom. Being of use is the spirit of the theological pastor who desires to encourage his people to greater Christlikeness through reliance on God's Spirit and word.

21 Augustine, *Sermons 306–340A*, 9:293.

Cultivating Friendships

This kind of theological pastor also needs good friends. Part of our (Coleman's and Shawn's) desire in writing this book was to work on a project together. For a season, we both labored alongside each other in doctoral studies, growing in friendship through our mutual love of theology and early Christianity. Countless hours spent in coffee shops, seminary classrooms, and church worship forged a bond between us. The idea of friendship even drove me (Coleman) toward my dissertation writing, focusing on the theology and practice of friendship in Augustine's life and thought. For Augustine, friendship was a vehicle for establishing and developing Christlike virtue in both parties.

Like us, Augustine also dealt with the stresses of a busy pastoral schedule. He preached multiple times a week, corresponded with various leaders, conversed with other clergy, and met with parishioners. In the late fourth and early fifth centuries, bishops also had civic duties such as hearing and deciding on local judicial matters. Pastors were public figures, perhaps even more so than today, because of their local visibility and the close connection between church and state. Augustine himself lamented the need to participate in civil affairs, often at the expense of more spiritual pursuits. His biographer Possidius recounted that while Augustine fulfilled this duty willingly, "this work . . . took him away from better things. . . . His greatest pleasure was always found in the things of God, or in the exhortation or conversation of intimate brotherly friendship."[22]

---

22 Possidius, *Life of St. Augustine*, in *Early Christian Biographies: Lives of St. Cyprian, St. Ambrose, St. Augustine, St. Anthony, St. Athanasius, St. Paul the First Hermit, St. Jerome, St. Epiphanius, with a Sermon on the Life of St. Honoratus*, trans. Roy J. Deferrari et al., Fathers of the Church 15 (Washington, DC: Catholic University of America Press, 1954), 19.

Thus, though busy with the realities of ministry and local leadership, Augustine always made time to discuss theology with his friends. In fact, he saw friendship as key to growth in Christlike virtue and theological growth.[23] It complemented—rather than hindered—theological development. This might be especially true for friendships between individuals who disagree on the finer points of theology, though that does not diminish the importance of friendships with like-minded believers. As previously mentioned, Augustine often corresponded with Paulinus of Nola (354–431), a capable theologian and poet. In a letter to Augustine, Paulinus commented on how well he had gotten to know Augustine just based on his books and letters. Asking to be further equipped theologically, Paulinus requested, "By your words teach me like someone still an infant with regard to the word of God and like someone still a nursling in terms of spiritual age as I reach for your breasts filled with faith, wisdom, and love."[24] Paulinus and Augustine's exchanges about theological and spiritual matters continued for many years. Though they never met face-to-face, they experienced the other's presence through letters.

Another of Augustine's friends was Alypius. We see their friendship forged in *Confessions*, continue in Augustine's early dialogues, and remain active through their correspondence together. Both entered the ministry around the same time, and both depended on one another for spiritual support for the remainder of their lives.

Many beautiful examples of their friendship are seen in Augustine's writings. One comes from the early dialogues of Augustine, written within the first year of his post-conversion yet pre-baptized

---

23 For more on friendship in Augustine's letters see Ford, *Bond between Souls*.

24 Saint Augustine, *Letters 1–99*, ed. John E. Rotelle, trans. Roland Teske, The Works of Saint Augustine: A Translation for the 21st Century (Hyde Park, NY: New City, 2001), 2:76.

life, making them his first Christian works. Augustine wrote during a philosophical retreat with friends at an Italian villa named Cassiciacum (modern-day Cassago Brianza), where he, Alypius, and the others discussed philosophical theories of happiness and knowledge. Overall, they saw theological development as a task done with friends and demonstrate how our theological minds often develop best in conversation with others.

Alypius continued to partner with Augustine in ministry amid the Donatist debate and sided with him during the Pelagian controversy. Though they came from the same hometown, it was more than a community connection that bonded these two souls together: it was a mutual love for the gospel and one another. To Augustine Alypius was nothing less than his "heart's brother."[25]

Conclusion

Like Augustine, pastors today also have busy ministry schedules, but prioritizing theological growth will always produce a healthy return on their investment. To do this, they must continually wrestle with theological topics—starting with God, the prime reality—in order to develop a rich inner life and clearly articulate complex truths for diverse individuals in their congregation. They can also benefit from being mentored by other pastors and theologians and developing friendships with fellow believers, as theology is meant to be done in community. Overall, the study of God is not reserved solely for academies and textbooks; it rightly belongs to the pastor and his people.

---

25 Augustine, *Confessions* 9.4.7. For more on the relationship between Alypius and Augustine, particularly in the letters of Augustine, see Ford, *Bond between Souls*, 116–24.

8

The Trinitarian Pastor and Gregory of Nazianzus

The three, one God, when contemplated together; each God because consubstantial; one God because of the monarchy

GREGORY OF NAZIANZUS

For us there is one God, the Father, from whom are all things and for whom we exist, and one Lord, Jesus Christ, through whom are all things and through whom we exist.

I CORINTHIANS 8:6

AFTER TAKING A CHURCH CLASS on the Trinity, a church member said to me (Shawn), "Learning about the Trinity is like walking through the wardrobe into Narnia." A sense of mystery and wonder meet Christians when they step through the Trinitarian wardrobe for the first time because God is the great mystery of Christian theology and the central confession of the Christian tradition. Once believers see the first few lampposts, they realize they are about to embark on an amazing journey that will forever alter their lives.

But if God is eternally mysterious, to what extent can we know him and help others know him? Pragmatism often governs our answer. Do we even have the time to consider this topic more deeply? Is the Trinity practical or useful? Early in my ministry, I decided to preach through Job, and one lesson I learned deeply affected me: when trials and suffering overwhelm you, rest in a God who self-reveals. Near the end of this book, God reveals himself to Job, but he offers little insight into the meaning of suffering, bypassing reasons for why it happens and instead speaking of his greater purposes. This taught me that in order to minister to suffering Christians, pastors need to know more about God.

When reflecting on their training in Trinitarian doctrine, many ministers express grief and remorse. Though they may have learned much about the Christian life, they were never taught about God's nature and feel they missed out on knowing God more fully. Further, reflecting on divine mystery does not fit easily into the schedule of a busy pastor or church, especially when pragmatism or anti-intellectualism has already gained a foothold. Unfortunately, many evangelical philosophies of ministry unknowingly create challenges for cultivating theological reflection. In addition to this, the complexity of theological categories and limits of human language can make the doctrine of the Trinity seem inaccessible.

Yet, none of this should scare us away; it should invite us in. God is not fully knowable, but we can still learn much about him. The innumerable amount of theology books written over hundreds of years—some of which we've seen in preceding chapters—show us that. And if we find our church has been infected by pragmatism or anti-intellectualism, we cannot stand by and watch it flounder. We have a responsibility to help.

Our plea to pastors is to abandon forms of utilitarianism in ministry and commit to being formed by and teach according to the classical doctrine of the Trinity. This can be accomplished in numerous ways such as adding a sermon or lesson that aligns with the church calendar (e.g., Trinity Sunday and Pentecost Sunday), all of which can add up over time. Because discipleship is a lifelong endeavor, we need to have a long-term approach to instilling Trinitarian doctrine in our own hearts and the hearts of our people. The doctrine of the Trinity requires a slow walk for a long while before we begin to see the ineffable wonder of God, and each step along the way it will support the health of our church.

Trinitarian Grammar: How to Speak Trinitarianly

The first step in seeing the wonder of the Trinity is learning what that word means and how to talk about God as Trinity. This is where classical Trinitarian grammar comes in to aid us—it teaches the tradition's language, which helps us communicate biblical doctrine effectively. Let's discuss a few of these concepts now.[1]

The Creator-Creature Distinction

One primary concept is the distinction between creature and Creator—God is wholly different and distinct from creation.[2] This

---

1   For more on Trinitarian grammar, see Gilles Emery, *The Trinitarian Theology of St Thomas Aquinas*, trans. Francesca Aran Murphy (Oxford: Oxford University Press, 2007); D. Glenn Butner, Jr., *Trinitarian Dogmatics: Exploring the Grammar of the Christian Doctrine of God* (Grand Rapids, MI: Baker Academic, 2022); Scott R. Swain, *The Trinity: An Introduction*, Short Studies in Systematic Theology (Wheaton, IL: Crossway, 2020).

2   The aseity of God, which is a subcategory with this Creator-creature distinction, is understood as God being "not from another" but "of himself God" or "life in and of himself." Steven J.

Creator-creature distinction is quite significant because the Scriptures often use human analogies to portray divine realities, but these analogies must not be understood as one-to-one comparisons between the human and divine. For example, to say "God is love" (1 John 4:16) is not to communicate that God is the greatest version of love in the human sense but that God is love in a totally different sense. Peter Sanlon explains,

> It is far from obvious that it should be easy for creatures to communicate with the Creator. Communication requires some common ground and capacity to comprehend the other. The Creator is infinite, perfect, timeless, free and omnipotent. Creatures are finite, imperfect, temporal, dependent and limited. The differences between the Creator and creature are so great that they pose significant obstacles to communication.[3]

All language about God will invariably fail to describe the divine life properly. The best we have is finite, human language to describe an infinite and mysterious God. But however we describe God cannot be solely based on human nature, activity, or experiences. Thus, we need to push ourselves to think outside human categories.

The Person-Nature Distinction, Eternal Generation, and Inseparable Operations

The pro-Nicene tradition did just that by coming up with ways to explain big biblical and philosophical ideas regarding the nature and

---

Duby, *Divine Simplicity: A Dogmatic Account*, T&T Clark Studies in Systematic Theology 30 (London: T&T Clark, 2016), 109; John Webster, *God Without Measure: Working Papers in Christian Theology*, T&T Clark Theology (London: T&T Clark, 2015), 13–28.

3 Peter Sanlon, *Simply God: Recovering the Classical Trinity* (Nottingham: Inter-Varsity Press, 2014), 23.

persons of God, the eternal generation of the Son, and the inseparable operations of the Father, Son, and Spirit.[4] The Nicene Creed (325) did not explicitly express all of these, but it did produce a theological culture by the mid- to late fourth century that led theologians like Gregory of Nazianzus to further develop such Trinitarian ideas. According to Lewis Ayres, three shared principles of this tradition are

1. a clear version of the person and nature distinction, entailing the principle that whatever is predicated of the divine nature is predicated of the three persons equally and understood to be one (this distinction may or may not be articulated via a consistent technical terminology);
2. clear expression that the eternal generation of the Son occurs within the unitary and incomprehensible divine being;
3. clear expression of the doctrine that the persons work inseparably.[5]

In other words, God is one nature and thus this nature applies to all three persons of the Trinity, the Son has no beginning and therefore there was never a time when the Son was not, and the persons of the Trinity are indivisible and thus all act together even though the Scriptures speak of the Father, Son, and Spirit doing particular acts.

The Theology-Economy Distinction

Another important concept in our Trinitarian grammar is the distinction between the theology of God (his eternal, interior life)

---

4 This section is a modified version of Shawn J. Wilhite, "What Does It Mean to Be 'Pro-Nicene'? The Development of Pro-Nicene Theology," *Credo Magazine* 10, no. 4 (2020). Used by permission.

5 Ayres, *Nicaea and Its Legacy: An Approach to Fourth-Century Trinitarian Theology* (Oxford: Oxford University Press, 2006), 236.

and economy of God (his exterior actions with the created realm, which flow from his interior life). In the classical tradition, theology refers to "pure theology" or God relating to nothing but Godself. It is this mysterious inner life of God that remains inaccessible and incomprehensible to us. Economy, on the other hand, refers to the outworking of God's missions and activities in the world, such as his revelation to creation and, more specifically, the active sending of the Son in the incarnation and the Spirit at Pentecost.[6]

Origen of Alexandria was among the first Christian theologians to use these two terms to describe God. He wrote that God speaks "theologically about himself and [not about] his plan [i.e., economy] for human matters."[7] Later, Basil applied these terms to Scriptural exegesis, writing, "Everyone who has paid even marginal attention to the intent of the Apostle's text recognizes that he does not teach us in the mode of theology, but hints at the reasons of the economy."[8]

While the Gospels and Acts display the economy and missions of the Son and the Spirit more prominently, pastors should look for both theology and economy while reading the Old and New Testaments. When a text highlights God's nature, reflect on the eternal life of God. When a text highlights God's activity, reflect on the external acts of God. And when speaking about God to others, try to convey both features to follow the logic of Nicaea: begin with theology and move toward economy.

6 Emery, *Trinity*, 199, 202.

7 Origen, *Homilies on Jeremiah* 18.6.3 in *Origen: Homilies on Jeremiah, Homily on 1 Kings 28*, trans. John Clark Smith, Fathers of the Church 97 (Washington, DC: The Catholic University of America Press, 1998). Lewis Ayres, "Pro-Nicene Theology: Theologia and Oikonomia," Zondervan Academic, December 1, 2016, https://zondervanacademic.com/.

8 St. Basil of Caesarea, *Against Eunomius*, trans. Mark DelCogliano and Andrew Radde-Gallwitz, Fathers of the Church 122 (Washington, DC: The Catholic University of America Press, 2011), 2.3.

Trinitarian Exegesis: How to Read Trinitarianly

Overall, using Trinitarian grammar will help us exegete Scripture. It is not an imposition on the text but reflects its core message. This means we must observe Trinitarian activity in the Bible from the start, using Christ as our interpretive key.

Seeing the Trinity in All of Scripture

Starting in Genesis 1, we see the work of the triune God. But the distinct acts of the persons of the Trinity are not necessarily explicit. This is where something called prosopological exegesis can help us. This type of interpretation identifies the Trinitarian persons in passages that do not name the Father, Son, and Spirit by reading the Scripture's vague pronouns as active agents. The fathers used this reading practice to arrive at orthodox Christology, ecclesiology, and pneumatology.[9]

Madison Pierce has brilliantly displayed the Scriptural basis for prosopology in Hebrews, showing how it underscores much of the author's argument.[10] Hebrews 1 provides several examples for us to consider. When Psalm 2:7 is cited in Hebrews 1:5—"You are my Son, today I have begotten you"—the unnamed pronouns refer to

---

9 Madison N. Pierce, *Divine Discourse in the Epistle to the Hebrews: The Recontextualization of Spoken Quotations in Scripture*, Society for New Testament Studies 178 (Cambridge: Cambridge University Press, 2020); Matthew W. Bates, *The Hermeneutics of the Apostolic Proclamation: The Center of Paul's Method of Scripture Interpretation* (Waco, TX: Baylor University Press, 2012); Matthew W. Bates, *The Birth of the Trinity: Jesus, God, and Spirit in New Testament and Early Christian Interpretations of the Old Testament* (Oxford: Oxford University Press, 2015); Kyle R. Hughes, *How the Spirit Became God: The Mosaic of Early Christian Pneumatology* (Eugene, OR: Cascade Books, 2020); Kyle R. Hughes, *The Trinitarian Testimony of the Spirit: Prosopological Exegesis and the Development of Pre-Nicene Pneumatology*, Supplements to Vigilae Christianae 147 (Leiden: Brill, 2018); Adam Ployd, "Pro-Nicene Prosopology and the Church in Augustine's Preaching on John 3:13," *Scottish Journal of Theology* 67, no. 3 (2014): 253–64.

10 Pierce, *Divine Discourse*.

the Father. "My" and "I" refer to the Father, and "you" refers to the Son. In light of this passage, a prosoponic reading of Hebrews then leads interpreters to insert the Trinitarian persons into Hebrews 1:5 (quoting 2 Sam. 7:14), "I will be to him a father, and he shall be to me a son," as God the Father speaking to Christ.

Christ as Our Interpretive Key

Overall, Christ is the key to unlocking the meaning of the Bible's big narrative. In the Harry Potter novels, a particular ominous figure always seems to be working against the young wizard—Professor Severus Snape. But in the end, when the villain Voldemort is about to kill Snape, we receive a vital part of the story: Snape was actually trying to protect Harry because he loved Harry's mother— "always."[11] Until this plot twist, most readers see Snape as an antagonistic character in cahoots with Voldemort himself. But once the key to Snape's true nature is revealed, readers see him in an entirely different light. Rereading the Harry Potter stories is thus an entirely different experience from reading them the first time.

Similarly, Christ is the interpretive key for the entirety of the Scriptures. Once we discover the risen Christ, we are invited to read the whole story of the Scriptures differently. I (Coleman) remember teaching a hermeneutics class in church when a member approached me after the first lesson. He was a longtime believer and served in various leadership roles within the church. I had started the class by unpacking Luke 24 as the way we are to read Scripture, and he confessed that he had never heard this before. Though he probably had read Luke 24 a dozen times, he never realized Jesus was informing us how to read our Bibles in light of his person and

11   J. K. Rowling, *Harry Potter and the Deathly Hallows* (New York: Scholastic, 2007), 687.

work. He then learned that Jesus provided a new way of reading, one that was grounded in his resurrection and was thus a distinctly Christian way of reading.

At the beginning of Luke 24, two people walk toward a village named Emmaus (v. 13). They are conversing about Jesus, hoping he was the one to redeem Israel (vv. 15, 19–21). Then Jesus appears to them, discusses the necessity of his sufferings, and shows them all that all of Scripture was about him (vv. 25–27). After he breaks bread, blesses it, and gives it to the travelers, they realize who he is (v. 31).

The rest of Luke 24 tells a similar story. Here, Jesus appears among a small crowd and the remaining eleven disciples while they are discussing the empty tomb, and they become frightened when they see him (v. 37). Then, Jesus provides a hermeneutical approach to reading the Old Testament (vv. 44–45) while they eat fish together.

As you can see, these stories are symmetrical. They both present the disciples' negative responses to Jesus, an echo of the Eucharist, and a Christocentric explanation of the Old Testament, and then a clearer understanding of Jesus emerges. While eating together, the disciples recognized and worshipped the resurrected Lord. Overall, this pattern tells us that good readings of Scripture occur in the life and practice of the church when they use the Son as their interpretive key. It teaches us to reread familiar stories of the Old Testament as stories about Christ.

Another patristic method of interpretation that helps us further refine our reading of Christ in Scripture is partitive (or two-nature) exegesis, which determines how to speak about Christological texts in light of the Son's dual natures (divine and human).[12] In sum,

---

12 John Behr provides a more detailed definition: "The issue between Nicenes and the non-Nicenes is a matter of exegesis. Both sides took Scripture as speaking of Christ. The non-Nicenes,

partitive exegesis limits language about the Son by prohibiting the division of his personhood. Instead, it uses a theology-economy framework to interpret Christological texts as referring to a single Son acting indivisibly by virtue of one of his natures. For example, a partitive reading of the Son's ignorance in Matthew 24 prohibits saying that he is partially omniscient and would rather say that the single Son is ignorant in his humanity and omniscient in his divinity. Similarly, a partitive reading of his perception of human hearts in John 2:23–25 would say that while the single Son appears in his human form, he knows all the thoughts and intentions of the human heart according to what befits his divine nature. Overall, partitive exegesis shows people how to read Christological texts in a way that appropriately identifies which activities are properly attributed to the divine eternal Son and the human incarnate Son.

---

however, insisted on an absolutely univocal exegesis, which applied all scriptural affirmations in a unitary fashion to one subject, who thus turns out to be a demi-god, neither fully divine nor fully human—created but not as one of the creatures. And, at least in the modern reading of this, this demi-god is a temporal being, which his own history—the 'preincarnate Logos' who eventually, as one phase in his existence, animate a body, becoming the man Jesus Christ. For the Nicenes, on the other hand, Scripture speaks throughout of Christ, but the Christ of the Kerygma, the crucified and exalted Lord, and speaks of him in a twofold fashion, demanding in turn a "partitive" exegesis: some things are said of him as divine and other things are said of him as human—yet referring to the same Christ throughout. Seen in this way, the conflict turns upon two different ways of conceptualizing the identity of Christ." John Behr, *The Nicene Faith*, vol. 1 of *Formation of Christian Theology* (Crestwood, NY: St. Vladimir's Seminary Press, 2004), 14. For use of this method in Cyril of Alexandria, see Shawn J. Wilhite, "Cyril of Alexandria's Trinitarian Exegesis" (PhD thesis, Durham University, 2022); Shawn J. Wilhite, " 'Was It Not the Only Begotten That Was Speaking Long Ago': Cyril of Alexandria's Christological Exegesis in His Commentary on Hebrews (Heb. 1:1–2)" *Studia Patristica* 129 (2021): 39–50. For its relation to the Chalcedonian Creed, see R. B. Jamieson and Tyler R. Wittman, *Biblical Reasoning: Christological and Trinitarian Rules for Exegesis* (Grand Rapids, MI: Baker Academic, 2022). "Scripture speaks of Christ in a twofold manner: some things are said of him as divine, and other things are said of him as human. Biblical reasoning discerns that Scripture speaks of the one Christ in two registers in order to contemplate the whole Christ. Therefore read Scripture in such a way that you discern the different registers in which Scripture speaks of Christ, yet without dividing him." Jamieson and Wittman, *Biblical Reasoning*, 153.

Gregory of Nazianzus

Gregory of Nazianzus (c. 325–390) provides an excellent, real-life model for us of how to speak and read Trinitarianly, especially for pastors, whose speaking is often preaching and reading is often exegeting. Gregory was born into an affluent, landowning family, and soon after his birth, his father, Gregory the Elder, became bishop of Nazianzus. Thus young Gregory was raised in and around the ministry of the church. Gregory began his studies in 342 with Carterios and Amphilocius the Elder and spent fifteen years pursuing education while he traveled from Cappadocian Caesarea to Palestinian Caesarea, Alexandria, and finally Athens.[13] From 348 to 355, he lived in Athens and began an intimate friendship with Basil of Caesarea. Gregory also befriended Basil's brother, Gregory of Nyssa, and the trio would later be referred to as the Cappadocian fathers. Near the end of 348, Gregory survived a three-week storm on his voyage to Athens even though he thought he was going to die.[14]

Gregory was installed in official church roles five times but fled from each of them shortly thereafter. It all began on Christmas Day, 361, when his father ordained him as presbyter or priest.[15] Stricken with panic, young Gregory fled to Basil's monastic estates. He returned a few months later and delivered his *Apology for his*

---

13 Brian E. Daley, *Gregory of Nazianzus*, Early Church Fathers (London: Routledge, 2006), 4–6.

14 See Gregory *On His Own Life* and *On His Own Affairs*, esp. 307–22 in *St. Gregory of Nazianzus: Three Poems: Concerning His Own Affairs, Concerning Himself and the Bishops, and Concerning His Own Life*, trans. Denis Molaise Meehan, Fathers of the Church 75 (Washington, DC: The Catholic University of America Press, 1987).

15 John McGuckin, *Saint Gregory of Nazianzus: An Intellectual Biography* (Crestwood, NY: St Vladimir's Seminary Press, 2001), 101; Susanna Elm, *Sons of Hellenism, Fathers of the Church: Emperor Julian, Gregory of Nazianzus, and the Vision of Rome*, Transformation of the Classical Heritage 49 (Berkeley, CA: University of California Press, 2012), 148.

Flight to Pontus and On the Priesthood,[16] but he fled once more to Basil by the winter of 363.[17]

In 372, Basil, along with Gregory's father, urged and appointed Gregory to become bishop of Sasima and he again fled the pastoral ordination, citing his desire for a contemplative life.[18] Yet, in 373, Gregory returned to be with his aging father. After his father's death (374), Gregory assumed the bishopric duties at Nazianzus. He then fled to a women's monastic community in Seleucia, where his sister Gorgonia lived.[19]

In 379, after the death of Basil, Gregory returned to oversee matters in Constantinople. In the midst of the Apollinarianism debate, he composed his *Five Theological Orations*, which earned him the title "the Theologian."[20] Shortly after the start of the Council of Constantinople, Gregory assumed its chair, and from 382 to 383, he moved back to Nazianzus to oversee his father's church for a second time.

So why did Gregory initially flee in 362? In short, he was afraid, and this caused him to lose control and self-respect. He wrote, "First, and most important, I was astounded at the unexpectedness of what had occurred, as people are terrified by sudden noises; and, losing the control of my reasoning faculties, my self-respect, which

16 Elm, *Sons of Hellenism*, 153.
17 "Like an ox stricken by the gadfly I made for Pontus, anxious to have the most godly of my friends as medicine for my agitation. For there, hidden in that cloud, like one of the sages of old, practicing union with God, was Basil, who is now with the angels. With him I soothed my agony of spirit." St. Gregory of Nazianzus, *Three Poems*, trans. Denis Molaise Meehan, Fathers of the Church 75 (Washington, DC: Catholic University of America Press, 1986), 350–56. In this quote we see two features of friendship: as medicine for mental illness and comfort for an aching heart.
18 Denis Molaise Meehan, *St. Gregory of Nazianzus*, 490–91.
19 Brian E. Daley, *Gregory of Nazianzus*, The Early Church Fathers (London: Routledge, 2006), 13.
20 Daley, *Gregory of Nazianzus*, 17.

had hitherto controlled me, gave way."[21] Gregory also wanted to experience the calmness of contemplating God. Pastoral work brings turmoil, and he desired to pursue God unencumbered by other experiences. He continued,

> In the next place, there came over me an eager longing for the blessings of calm and retirement, of which I had from the first been enamoured to a higher degree, I imagine, than any other student of letters, and which amidst the greatest and most threatening dangers I had promised to God, and of which I had also had so much experience, that I was then upon its threshold, my longing having in consequence been greatly kindled, so that I could not submit to be thrust into the midst of a life of turmoil by an arbitrary act of oppression, and to be torn away by force from the holy sanctuary of such a life as this.[22]

According to Gregory, to pursue this office one had to be filled with virtue because the guiding of souls was "the art of arts and science of sciences."[23] Brian Daley reflects well on the final portions of Gregory's life: "As Gregory declined into old age, style and language, preaching and politics, the discipline of virtue and the pursuit of contemplation, all fused into a single preoccupation. The complexity of his life had itself become a work of art."[24]

---

21 Gregory of Nazianzus, *Oration* 2.6 in *Nicene and Post-Nicene Fathers, Second Series*, vol. 7, trans. Charles Gordon Browne and James Edward Swallow (Peabody, MA: Hendrickson, 1994).

22 Gregory, *Oration* 2.6.

23 Gregory, *Oration* 2.16.

24 Daley, *Gregory of Nazianzus*, 26.

Preaching Trinitarianly

As seen in his fascinating life story, Gregory suffered under the pressures of pastoral work, but he flourished when thinking about God, and this greatly influenced his writing and preaching. In the opening of *Oration* 28, he argued that pastors must preach Trinitarian theology in order to ascend to the heights of God and provide cleansing teaching for the church. He explained,

> Last time we used theology to cleanse the theologian. We glanced at his character, his audience, the occasion and range of his theorizing. We saw that his character should be undimmed, making for a perception of light by light; that his audience should be serious-minded, to ensure that the word shall be no sterile sowing in serial ground; that the right occasion is when we own an inner stillness away from the outward whirl, avoiding all fitful checks to the spirit; and that the range should be that of our God-given capacity.[25]

In addition to this ethical purity, preaching on the Trinity brings pastors and their churches on a spiritual ascent to God similar to the ascent Moses took to Mount Sinai to see the mysteries of God's presence. Gregory explained, "I eagerly ascend the mount—or, to speak truer, ascend in eager hope matched with anxiety for my frailty—that I may enter cloud and company with God (for such is God's bidding)."[26] Then, Gregory asked who his listeners identified with. Was anyone Aaron, Nadab, an animal

---

25 Gregory, *Oration* 28.1. St. Gregory of Nazianzus, *On God and Christ: The Five Theological Orations and Two Letters to Cledonius*, trans. Frederick Williams and Lionel Wickham, Popular Patristics Series 23 (Crestwood, NY: St Vladimir's Seminary Press, 2002).

26 Gregory, *Oration* 28.2.

on the mountain, or the crowd below? The kind of person who accompanied Moses was hidden in the rock, the incarnate Christ. As the eighteenth-century hymn writer Augustus Toplady expressed centuries later,

> Rock of ages, cleft for me,
> let me hide myself in thee;
> let the water and blood,
> from Thy wounded side which flowed
> be of sin the double cure;
> save from wrath and make me pure.[27]

In Christ, we are saved and purified; in Christ, we can contemplate the beauties of God and his redemptive work. And contemplating God ultimately changes the vision and character of the community of God.

But what exactly should one preach about the Trinity? Gregory's *Theological Orations* show us just that. This collection of five discourses centered on a theological vision of God and teaches us the basics of Trinitarian theology.[28] First, Gregory argued that God does not have a body. For God to be infinite, he must be incorporeal, meaning simple or non-composite.[29] Further, he is properly ingenerate, unoriginate, immutable, and immortal.[30] Here, Gregory used both cataphatic (positive) and apophatic (negative)

---

27 Augustus Toplady, "Rock of Ages" (1776).

28 *Oration* 28 focuses on God and the divine life, *Orations* 29 to 30 on the Son, and *Oration* 31 on the Holy Spirit.

29 "For composition is cause of conflict, conflict of division, division of dissolution. But dissolution is utterly alien to God the prime nature. So no dissolution means no division; no division means no conflict; no conflict means no composition, and hence no body involving composition." Gregory, *Oration* 28.7.

30 Gregory, *Oration* 28.9.

descriptions. The former identifies what God is and the latter identifies what God is not. Both are required because though we can know God, we cannot fully understand him.[31]

The Theologian then described God as the "prime reality."[32] Though the prime reality is non-corporeal and invisible to the human eye, he assumes physical features and uses "sight as a guide to what transcends sight without losing God through the grandeur of what it sees."[33] This "sight" of God is spiritual and an even more beautiful way to contemplate him.

Gregory further explained that God's names, relations, and processions are eternal and nontemporal. Whereas humans relate within time, the processions of the Son and Spirit from the Father are outside of time. The names of God show this: the Father is "Ingenerate," the Son is "Begotten," and the Spirit is the one who "Proceeds from the Father."[34] Though the category of "when" does not technically apply to the Son's and Spirit's temporal origins, Gregory said that if one must know when, it was concurrent to

---

31 "So, in the same way, an inquirer into the nature of a real being cannot stop short of saying what it is *not* but must add to his denials a positive affirmation (and how much easier it is to take in a single thing than to run the full gamut of particular negations!). . . . A person who tells you what God is not but fails to tell you what he is, is rather like someone who, asked what twice five are, answers 'not two, not three, not four, not five, not twenty, not thirty, no number, in short, under ten or over ten.'" Gregory, *Oration* 28.9.

32 Gregory, *Oration* 28.13.

33 Gregory, *Oration* 28.13.

34 "For this reason, a one eternally changes to two and stops at three—meaning the Father, the Son, and the Holy Spirit. In a serene, non-temporal, incorporeal way, the Father is parent of the 'offspring' and the originator of the 'emanation'—or whatever name one can apply when one has entirely extrapolated from things visible. . . . We limit ourselves to Christian terms and speak of 'the Ingenerate,' 'the Begotten,' and (as God the Word himself does in one passage) 'what Proceeds from the Father.'" Gregory, *Oration* 29.2. While Gregory appeared to suggest that God is mutable, he actually offered a rhetorical rebuttal to polytheism and atheism by further explaining that one person changes to two persons and then three persons.

when the Father originated.[35] As there has never been a time when the Father has not been Father, the Son has likewise always been begotten and the Spirit has always proceeded. Thus, being begotten and proceeding from do not mean being created. The Son is still immutable and possesses all the divine properties of the Father, which means the Father has never been without the Son (indeed, his very name assumes an offspring). Gregory referred to over 120 scriptures to show this.[36]

Similarly, the Spirit was not created. What is said about the Father and the Son must also be said about the Spirit because the three equally, without division, and eternally have the same nature.[37] If one person had a beginning, all three persons would have a beginning. And a person who comes after another is inferior. But the eternal processions are atemporal. Thus, the Spirit is glorified with the Father and the Son without any partial division of the one God or a composite of three deities; one person is not superior to the other, nor do they outdo one another in honor.[38]

---

35 "If there was a 'when' when the Father did not exist, there was a 'when' when the Son did not exist. If there was a 'when' when the Son did not exist, there was a 'when' when the Holy Spirit did not exist. If one existed from the beginning, so did all three. If you cast one down, I make bold to tell you not to exalt the other two." Gregory, *Oration* 31.4.

36 Gregory, *Oration* 29.17–21.

37 "For our part we have such confidence in the Godhead of the Spirit, that, rash though some may find it, we shall begin our theological exposition by applying identical expressions to the Three. 'He was the true light that enlightens every man coming into the world' (John 1:9)—yes, the Father. 'He was the true light that enlightens every man coming into the world'—yes, the Son. 'He was the true light that enlightens every man coming into the world'—yes, the Comforter. These are the three subjects and three verbs—he was and he was and he was. But a single reality was. There are three predicates—light and light and light. But the light is one, God is one." Gregory, *Oration* 31.3.

38 "Though there are three objects of belief, they derive from the single whole and have reference to it. They do not have degrees of being God or degrees of priority over against one another. . . . To express it succinctly, the Godhead exists undivided in being divided." Gregory, *Oration* 31.14.

Overall, Gregory aligned the Spirit with the Father and Son as coequal, consubstantial, and co-temporal.

Exegeting Trinitarianly

Just as Gregory can help us preach Trinitarianly, so can he help us exegete Trinitarianly by using partitive exegesis. He wrote,

> In sum: you must predicate the more sublime expressions of the Godhead, of the nature which transcends bodily experiences, and the lowlier ones of the compound, of him who because of you was emptied, became incarnate and (to use equally valid language) was "made man." Then next he was exalted, in order that you might have done with the earthbound carnality of your opinions and might learn to be nobler, to ascend with the Godhead and not linger on in things visible but rise up to spiritual realities, and that you might know what belongs to his nature and what to God's plan of salvation.[39]

Overall, Gregory's partitive exegesis presumes several interpretive and theological commitments: (1) a theology-economy framework, (2) a combined use of scriptural and creedal language (see "born in the likeness of men" in Phil. 2:7 and the Nicene Creed), (3) a commitment to the full career of the Son (eternal, incarnate, and exalted), (4) an observation of the two natures of a single Son, and (5) the spiritual ascent of the interpreter.

These commitments are seen throughout Gregory's *Theological Orations*. For example, Gregory partitively read Proverbs 8:22–25 to depict the eternal begetting and incarnation of the

---

39 Gregory, *Oration* 29.18

Son.[40] After commenting on the personification of wisdom, Gregory distinguished between begotten and created, writing, "The passage is now free of complication, seeing that we find there clearly both expressions 'created' and 'begets me.'"[41] To be begotten is an eternal activity of the Son, and to be created refers to the incarnation of the same Son. This partitive reading strategy differentiates between what is eternal and divine and what refers to the Son's entrance into the human realm.[42] In using this strategy, Gregory thus flipped an Arian argument on its head. Whereas Arius decades before had used Proverbs 8 to argue for the Son's temporal beginning, Gregory used the text to prove his eternality.

Gregory also used a partitive reading strategy for the cry of dereliction from Psalm 22:1 (see Matt. 27:46), "My God, my God, why have you forsaken me?" Here, he explained what the text cannot mean in order to say what it can mean. The Father and Spirit do not abandon the Son. In Gregory's words, "He is not forsaken either by the Father or, as some think, by his own Godhead, which shrank in fear from suffering, abandoning the sufferer. Who applies that argument either to his birth in this world in the first place or to his ascent of the cross?"[43] Instead, the incarnate Son on the cross cried forth to empathize with humanity. Gregory explained,

40 This text and reading strategy frequently appear in pro-Nicene writers. Lewis Ayres, "Scripture in the Trinitarian Controversies," in *The Oxford Handbook of Early Christian Biblical Interpretation*, ed. Paul M. Blowers and Peter W. Martens (Oxford: Oxford University Press, 2019), 439–54.

41 Gregory, *Oration* 30.2.

42 "Whatever we come across with a causal implication we will attribute to the humanity; what is absolute and free of cause we will reckon to the Godhead." Gregory, *Oration* 30.2.

43 Gregory, *Oration* 30.5.

In himself, as I have said, he expresses our condition. We had once been the forsaken and the disregarded; then we were accepted and now are saved by the sufferings of the impassible. He made our thoughtlessness and waywardness his own, just as the Psalm, in its subsequent course, says—since the Twenty-First Psalm clearly refers to Christ.[44]

A partitive reading of Matthew 27:46 situates the Son as sharing in our condition of being abandoned by God and speaking from our position. It does not refer to what is proper of the Son's eternal divine life but is the single Son's experience on the cross by virtue of assuming a full humanity.[45]

Gregory also used partitive exegesis when highlighting the Son's qualities in relation to the Father, citing two scriptures: the Father is "greater" than the Son (John 14:28), and the Son says to the Father, "my God and your God" (John 20:17). If the Son is eternal God with the Father, how should we understand these passages? They exclusively refer to the incarnate Son in relation to the Father by virtue of the Son's humanity. Gregory said, "Of course, the explanation that the Father is greater than the Son considered as man is true, but trivial. Is there anything remarkable about God's being greater than man? Certainly, this must be our answer to those who preen themselves on their 'being greater.'"[46]

To underscore this reading, Gregory cited several passages highlighting what is proper to the Son's nature. The Son receives "life" (John 5:26), "judgment" (John 5:22, 27), "inheritance of the

---

44 Gregory, *Oration* 30.5.

45 Other fathers such as Augustine followed this same exegetical pattern and had additional exegetical insights. See Hubertus R. Drobner, "Psalm 21 in Augustine's *Sermones ad populum*: Catecheses on *Christus totus* and Rules of Interpretation," *Augustinian Studies* 37, no. 2 (2006): 145–69.

46 Gregory, *Oration* 30.7.

Gentiles" (Ps 2:8), "power over all flesh" (John 17:2), "glory" (Rev 5:12), "disciples" (John 17:6), indeed, "everything,"[47] in his humanity. Gregory explained, "This 'receiving' belongs to his manhood. Yet it would not be absurd to ascribe it to the Godhead. You will not be ascribing him acquired properties, but properties which have existed with him from the outset, not by a principle of grace but by a condition of his nature."[48]

Overall, Gregory's use of partitive exegesis shows us that when we read about the human experiences of the Son in the Gospels, we must refrain from applying them to the eternal Son. The persons of the Trinity equally and without division share the same nature, so if the Son in the Gospels grows tired, experiences sorrow, or desires food and rest, we must ask, are these exclusive to the incarnate, human Son or are they proper to the godhead, equally and indivisibly shared by the three persons? We must not, for example, universalize the Son's ignorance about the timing of the recreation of the universe (Mark 13:32) as proper of the eternal Son because that would then imply that the Father and the Spirit are also ignorant. Partitive exegesis thus helps us avoid such exegetical and theological mistakes.

Conclusion

Dutch theologian Herman Bavinck argued that "in the confession of the Trinity we hear the heartbeat of the Christian religion: every error results from, or upon deeper reflection is traceable to, a departure in the doctrine of the Trinity."[49] The classical doctrine of

---

47 Gregory, *Oration* 30.9.
48 Gregory, *Oration* 30.9.
49 Herman Bavinck, *Reformed Dogmatics*, eds. John Bolt and John Vriend (Grand Rapids, MI: Baker Academic, 2004), 2:288.

the Trinity is the lifeblood of Christian life and ministry. When we stop to consider the doctrine of God, we see that it is not merely a theoretical exercise that leads into the great mystery of the Trinity but also a practical exercise that can lead us to teach and preach more effectively. The life of Gregory of Nazianzus proves that to us. Becoming a Trinitarian pastor in the spirit of Gregory does not require a PhD in dogmatics; it requires a humble heart willing to submit to the truth of God in Scripture. Only then will the men and women in our churches grow in their understanding of and devotion to God who is Father, Son, and Spirit.

PART 3

————————

THE MINISTRY
OF A PASTOR

9

The Contemplative Pastor
and Gregory the Great

The contemplative life is . . . to rest from exterior action and
cleave only to the desire of the maker, that the mind may
now take no pleasure in doing anything, but having spurned
all cares, may be aglow to see the face of the Creator.

GREGORY THE GREAT

For God alone my soul waits in silence.

PSALM 62:1

I (SHAWN) REMEMBER where I stood, who was with me, and the season—it was springtime because baseball had recently begun—when I stood in my study, reading Gregory the Great's *Pastoral Rule*. The double love command was fresh on my mind, and I could sense how Gregory was already shifting my vision of the pastoral office. I then read Eugene Peterson's *The Contemplative Pastor*. It was such a simple read, and I remember finishing it in a single day, unable to put it down. Peterson's vision of the office slowly melded together with Gregory's. This part of Peterson's book was not new to me, but it felt different that day:

> It was a favorite theme of C. S. Lewis that only lazy people work hard. By lazily abdicating the essential work of deciding and directing, establishing values and setting goals, other people do it for us; then we find ourselves frantically, at the last minute, trying to satisfy a half dozen different demands on our time, none of which is essential to our vocation, to stave off the disaster of disappointing someone. But if I vainly crowd my day with conspicuous activity or let others fill my day with imperious demands, I don't have time to do my proper work, the work to which I have been called. How can I lead people into the quiet place beside the still waters if I am in perpetual motion? How can I persuade a person to live by faith and not by works if I have to juggle my schedule constantly to make everything fit into place?[1]

As I read this, my soul grew unsettled, and I knew something was happening. Of course we need to plan for our day. Of course we have plenty of pastoral meetings and vocational meetings. Of course we have projects to finish, people to visit, and phone calls to make. But how do I create space in my schedule for my piety and stave off the demands of stuff?

For days afterward, Peterson's line reverberated throughout my soul: "How can I lead people into the quiet place beside the still waters if I am in perpetual motion?" Psalm 23 depicts God as a

---

1 Eugene H. Peterson, *The Contemplative Pastor: Returning to the Art of Spiritual Direction* (Grand Rapids, MI: Eerdmans, 1989), 19.

shepherd to David. He nurtures us. He leads us. He guides us. God is the one who leads us to still waters to drink deeply from the Father's presence, the goodness of the Son, and the peace of the Spirit.

We all know a frantic person, someone who chases something they cannot fully grasp. We can see their tired soul, the fatigue in their eyes, and their disordered inner life. They exude a sense of restlessness. Maybe this is what some of us see every morning when we look in the mirror. Does your life feel chaotic, as if you're running from one thing to the next? Are you leading people to the goodness of Christ while doubting his goodness yourself? Are you finding your soul fatigued while you perform good deeds? Do you neglect to cease from your labor and internal spinning to rest in God? In ministry, we do many good things in a single day or week—we pray, teach, counsel, tend to the needs of others, and care for widows. We may feel frantic because we have said yes to many good and noble ministry duties.

Working for the church can be good and noble; we should labor on behalf of people's souls. Yet, to labor without rest may be idolatry. It may also be a ministry that is lacking in spiritual depth, as we can care for others while empty, chasing fulfillment. The veneer of busyness and the drive for acceptance can govern our identity, clouding our well-being, our pursuit of spirituality, and our times of reflection.

The contemplative tradition—which began with the fathers and continues today—shows us that the desire for acceptance at any cost and the commitment to busyness without limits are spiritual vices. Augustine likened the human life to a pilgrimage that joins one's soul to God: we are constantly "called home from the noise that is around us to the joys that are silent. Why do we rush about . . . looking for God who is here at home with us, if all we want is to be with him?"[2] By slowing down, we draw closer to God.

In fact, by slowing down, we will also be more effective in ministry. Reflecting on lessons from Gregory the Great for Christian educators, Kyle Hughes says, "By tending to our own spiritual and emotional health, we will be better able to deal with inevitable things like conflict and tension both inside and outside the classroom, gradually becoming transformed into the kinds of people that we would want our students to emulate."[3] Whether a student in a classroom or a congregant in a sanctuary, our own spiritual lives matter to those whom we serve. The point is not to cease all ministerial duties but to put proper limits on ministerial work because we are human. Kelly Kapic clarifies, "Denying our finitude cripples us in ways we don't realize. It also distorts our view of God and what Christian spirituality should look like."[4] Thus, we must find time for rest in God in order to do effective ministry.

Spiritual Practices from the Contemplative Tradition

Spiritual practices from the contemplative tradition do not usually come easy to Western Christians today, but they can provide a much-needed corrective to our obsession with busyness. Here are some you can try:

Silence and solitude. Silence and solitude refer to both an internal and external reality that can tether your soul to the triune

---

2 John E. Rotelle, ed., *Saint Augustine: The Trinity (De Trinitate)*, The Works of Saint Augustine: A Translation for the 21st Century (Hyde Park, NY: New City, 2017), 8.7.11.

3 Kyle R. Hughes, *Teaching for Spiritual Formation: A Patristic Approach to Christian Education in a Convulsed Age* (Eugene, OR: Cascade Books, 2022), 21.

4 Kelly M. Kapic, *You're Only Human: How Your Limits Reflect God's Design and Why That's Good News* (Grand Rapids, MI: Brazos Press, 2022), 6.

God. These disciplines require voluntary action to withdraw temporarily to meet with God, be alone, and think deeply about God—his majesty and presence—and your personal life. Often, these two disciplines go together—they are sisters who never separate. Many fear silence and solitude because they perceive them as loneliness. Dallas Willard notes, "We find complete silence shocking because it leaves the impression that nothing is happening."[5] However, the opposite of silence and solitude is not busyness but isolation. When you are quiet and alone, it is then that you will meet God. As Richard Foster says, "Jesus calls us from loneliness to solitude."[6]

Resting in God. Augustine famously said in his *Confessions*, "You have made us for yourself, and our heart is restless until it rests in you."[7] Like a tired child climbing onto the lap of a loving father, contemplative Christians went to God for physical, emotional, mental, and spiritual rest. Rest can include sleeping, seeking safety, or freely expressing one's concerns. It can look different for each person and is a subjective experience.

Being conscious of the soul's union with God. Contemplative Christians intentionally sought stillness in their souls and oriented them around spiritual communion with God. This sounds mystical because it is—a mystical union between a human's finite spirit and the God of the universe.

Integrating emotions, experiences, and beliefs. Within our Protestant tradition, we tend to overemphasize reason and objectivity.

---

5 Dallas Willard, *The Spirit of the Disciplines: Understanding How God Changes Lives* (New York: HarperCollins, 1991), 163.

6 Richard J. Foster, *Celebration of Discipline: The Path to Spiritual Growth*, 3rd ed. (New York: HarperOne, 1998), 96.

7 Augustine, *Confessions*, trans. Henry Chadwick, Oxford World's Classics (Oxford: Oxford University Press, 1998), 1.1.

The contemplative tradition can help us regain an appreciation for our subjective spiritual experiences while not relinquishing our theological beliefs. For those who are uncomfortable discussing or cultivating such experiences, it can help to think of them as a subcategory of spirituality, which is a subcategory of theology. Such experiences are thus not antithetical to our theological beliefs but the very outworking of those beliefs in our personal lives.

Letting go of the desire for approval from others. Practices like Bible reading and memorization have visible checkmarks that others can see and applaud. But the contemplative tradition is fundamentally a solitary, inner experience and thus has little social payoff. No one can see your inner life or your inner peace with God. And unlike memorizing Scripture passages, you cannot objectively measure your successes or failures. But when you pray in secret, your heavenly Father "who sees in secret will reward you" (Matt. 6:6). In this secret place, you will experience true spirituality, the "surrendering of deeply embedded resistances that allow the sacred within gradually to reveal itself as a simple fundamental fact."[8]

What the Contemplative Tradition Is Not

As we've shown, Western Christians can sometimes misinterpret practices of the contemplative tradition like silence and solitude. To further protect you against such misunderstandings, here is a list of what the contemplative tradition is not:

Isolationism or monasticism. The contemplative tradition may seem individualistic and lacking in communal relationships, but it

8   M. S. Laird, *Into the Silent Land: A Guide to the Christian Practice of Contemplation* (Oxford: Oxford University Press, 2006), 8.

is actually the opposite. In his *Life Together*, Dietrich Bonhoeffer has two chapters entitled "The Day Together" and "The Day Alone," showing that community and solitude are essential, symbiotic components of the Christian life. He writes,

> Let him who cannot be alone beware of community. . . . Let him who is not in community beware of being alone. . . . Each by itself has profound pitfalls and perils. One who wants fellowship without solitude plunges into the voice of words and feelings, and one who seeks solitude without fellowship perishes in the abyss of vanity, self-infatuation, and despair.[9]

Similarly, Gregory the Great used the double love as a guide for the contemplative life. To love God, one must seek him in times of focus and withdrawal. To love neighbor, one must reenter society to love and engage others. Neither can be used to hide or retreat from the other. Thus, the contemplative tradition should not be confused with isolationism or monasticism, which often includes permanently removing oneself from society.

Exclusively Roman Catholic or Eastern Orthodox. Though the contemplative tradition is often represented by famous Catholic and Orthodox theologians, it is not inherently antithetical to Protestantism. In fact, many popular Protestant theologians embraced contemplative practices. Here are some examples:

> John Owen (1616–1683): "A second season calling for the exercise of our minds in thoughts of the omnipresence and omniscience of God is made up of our solitudes and retirements.

9　Dietrich Bonhoeffer, *Life Together: The Classic Exploration of Christian Community* (New York: HarperOne, 1978), 77–78.

These give us the most genuine trials whether we are spiritually minded or not. What we are in them, that we are, and no more."[10]

David Brainerd (1718–1747): "Withdrew to my usual place of retirement in great peace and tranquility, and spent about two hours in secret duties. I felt much as I did yesterday morning, only weaker and more overcome. I seemed to hang and depend wholly upon my dear Lord; wholly weaned from all other dependences. I knew not what to say to my God, but only lean on his bosom, as it were, and breathe out my desires after a perfect conformity to him in all things. Thirsting desires and insatiable longings possessed my soul after perfect holiness: God was so precious to my soul that the world with all its enjoyments was infinitely vile: I had no more value for the favor of men than for pebbles. The Lord was my all; and he overruled all; which greatly delighted me. I think my faith and dependence upon God scarce ever rose so high. I saw him such a fountain of goodness, that it seemed impossible I should distrust him again, or be any way anxious about anything that should happen to me."[11]

Jonathan Edwards (1703–1758): "True religion disposes persons to be much alone in solitary places, for holy meditation and prayer."[12]

C. H. Spurgeon: "Time spent in quiet prostration of soul before the Lord is most invigorating. . . . Quietude, which some men

---

10 John Owen, *The Works of John Owen*, ed. William H. Goold (Edinburgh: Banner of Truth, 1965), 7:375.

11 Jonathan Edwards, *The Life and Diary of David Brainerd*, vol. 7 of *The Works of Jonathan Edwards*, ed. Norman Pettit (New Haven, CT: Yale University Press, 1985), 165.

12 Jonathan Edwards, *On Religious Affections* in *Works* (Edinburgh: Banner of Truth, 1974), 2:312.

cannot abide, because it reveals their inner poverty, is as a palace of cedar to the wise, for along its hallowed courts the King in his beauty deigns to walk. . . . Priceless as the gift of utterance may be, the practice of silence in some aspects far excels it. Do you think me a Quaker? Well, be it so. Herein I follow George Fox most lovingly; for I am persuaded that most of us think too much of speech, which after all is but the shell of thought. Quiet contemplation, still worship, unuttered rapture, these are mine when my best jewels are before me. Brethren, rob not your heart of the deep sea joys; miss not the far-down life, by for ever babbling among the broken shells and foaming surges of the shore."[13]

Eastern mysticism. Thomas Keating, a Catholic monk, counters the idea that contemplation is levitation, emptying the mind, or practicing relaxation exercises.[14] The Christian contemplative tradition does not need to be associated with non-Christian mysticisms; it finds its origins in Christianity and does not owe anything to the spirituality of other religions.

Gregory the Great

Now that we have laid a foundation for what contemplative theology is and is not, we can look to Gregory the Great (540–604) as an example of the contemplative pastor. Gregory was born into an aristocratic Roman family that included a lineage of religious leaders: great-great-grandfather Pope Felix III (bishop of Rome from 483 to 492) and uncle Pope Agapetus (bishop of Rome from 533 to 536). Three of his aunts may have been estate-dwelling

13 C. H. Spurgeon, *Lectures to My Students* (Grand Rapids, MI: Zondervan, 1954), 51.
14 Thomas Keating, "What Contemplation Is Not," Contemplative Outreach, https://www.contemplativeoutreach.org/.

ascetics.[15] Gregory is known as Gregory the Great by Western Christians and Gregory the Dialogist by Eastern Christians. According to Robert Markus, Gregory read quite widely in the Latin tradition, and "in all essentials it was Augustine's conceptual structures that shaped the world of his imagination."[16]

By the time Gregory turned thirty-three, he had become the prefect of the city. Since his birth, control of Rome had switched three times between imperial and Gothic rule. Byzantine emperor Justinian and his armies finally warded off the Goths and established a permanent Eastern Roman influence at Ravenna in the 550s. In 568, the Lombards (a Germanic people group from northwestern and central Europe) crossed the Alps into Italy, further threatening the political rule in Rome.[17] It was during these shifting political threats that Gregory emerged as a public figure.

Gregory's tenure as prefect lasted only a year due to traumatic events such as the threat of the Lombards and the deaths of Pope John III and Byzantine general Narses. Gregory then retreated from public service to pursue the contemplative life of monasticism.[18] In 579, after living as a monk for five years, Pope Pelagius II appointed Gregory as a deacon and papal representative to the emperor in Constantinople.[19] Eventually, Gregory was selected to succeed Pelagius II as the bishop of Rome (590–604).

One of Gregory's greatest treatises was his *Book on Pastoral Rules*. George Demacopoulos notes that this book "is the most thorough

---

15 George E. Demacopoulos, *Gregory the Great: Ascetic, Pastor, and First Man of Rome* (Notre Dame, IN: University of Notre Dame Press, 2015), 1.

16 R. A. Markus, *Gregory the Great and His World* (Cambridge: Cambridge University Press, 1997), 40.

17 Demacopoulos, *Gregory the Great*, 1–2.

18 Demacopoulos, *Gregory the Great*, 2.

19 Demacopoulos, *Gregory the Great*, 3.

pastoral treatise of the Patristic era."[20] The *Pastoral Rule* includes instructions about the pastoral office and a chastened ascetic life from a mature bishop to a younger bishop. It has four parts, with the first two focusing on the spiritual attention that a pastor ought to pay to himself and the church, the third describing how a spiritual director ought to shepherd, and the fourth showing how the pastor should return to humility after public ministry.

Gregory stood between two worlds—ascetic contemplation of God and public ministry to the church—and thus the double love was important to his vision of a bishop. On the one hand, a pastor is to love God, and part of loving God is contemplating God. On the other hand, Christians must love their neighbors and thus cannot remain in an ascetic life. Demacopoulos explains that Gregory

> believed that successful pastoral leadership required a balance between the contemplation of the isolated ascetic and the action of the well-trained administrator. The "active-contemplative" was not only a more effective leader, he was also a better Christian than either the recluse or the administrator.[21]

Balancing Contemplation and Ministry

As seen above, Gregory envisioned two forms of life: the contemplative life and the active life. To contemplate God was to reflect on the mysteries of God and participate in the divine life of God. These still the soul and enable the minister to drink deeply from the well of God's presence. Yet, one must also engage in ministry. The two forms always go together—no one can properly minister to others

---

20 St. Gregory the Great, *The Book of Pastoral Rule*, trans. George E. Demacopoulos, Popular Patristics Series 34 (Crestwood, NY: St. Vladimir's Seminary Press, 2007), bk. 13.

21 Demacopoulos, "An Introduction for the Reader," 16.

if the quiet life is all-consuming, and no one can properly contemplate if ministry is all-consuming. Gregory thus called those entering the pastoral office to slow down and pursue a balanced life of contemplating God and ministry to others. He wrote,

> The spiritual director should be a compassionate neighbor to everyone and superior to all in contemplation so that he may transfer the infirmities of others to himself by means of his intense piety and transcend even his own aspirations for invisible things through the loftiness of his meditation. Otherwise, in pursuing high things he will despise the infirmities of his neighbors, or by adapting himself to the infirmities of his neighbors he will abandon the pursuit of high things.[22]

Thus, Gregory taught that even while contemplating God, pastors must act with compassion for their neighbors. To live a superior life of contemplation is a way to bear the sicknesses of the church. Retreating to the inner life ought not be a retreat from ministry; instead, one must retreat to the inner life only to return and minister to one's neighbor. Yet, Gregory counseled, "It is necessary that the attention that is given to the external concerns of the laity must be kept to a certain limit."[23]

Studying the Art of Arts

According to Gregory, pastors are those who have mastered soul care, which is the art of arts, through study. Proper study of this art is required in order to navigate its ever-moving and unpredictable waves. In his words, "No one presumes to teach an art that he has not first mastered through study. How foolish it is therefore for the

22 Gregory, *Pastoral Rule*, pt. 2, sec. 5.
23 Gregory, *Pastoral Rule* 2.7.

inexperienced to assume pastoral authority when the care of souls is the art of arts."[24] It takes time for pastors to hone their craft, and it takes time for others to trust them. Gregory used an image of a child running back to a mother for comfort to describe this relationship:

> But, those who preside over others should exhibit a type of behavior that will lead the laity to disclose their secrets to them. Consequently, when the weak endure the waves of temptation, they will return to their pastor's counsel as a crying child seeks its mother's breast. And in the solace of his counsel and the tears of prayer, the laity will cleanse themselves of the defilement of sin that attacks them.[25]

In other words, gospel ministers must care for parishioners in a way that makes them feel comforted, understood, and known as unique individuals. This will lead them to grow in trust of their minister. It will also cause them to more readily flee temptation and repent of sin, more fervently seek prayer, and find more meaningful solace in pastoral counsel.

The Pastor's Virtue

According to Gregory, this kind of soul care could only be done by a virtuous pastor. He wrote,

> It is necessary, therefore, that he should be pure in thought, exemplary in conduct, discerning in silence, profitable in speech, a compassionate neighbor to everyone, superior to all in contemplation, a humble companion to the good, and firm in the zeal of righteousness against the vices of sinners. He must not

24 Gregory, *Pastoral Rule* 1.1
25 Gregory, *Pastoral Rule* 2.5.

relax his care for the internal life while he is occupied by external concerns, nor should he relinquish what is prudent of external matters so as to focus on the things internal.[26]

Gregory then expanded on these virtues. First, the purity of the minister's thought life affects his ministry to the church. As the divine voice rested on Aaron and provided a vestment (cf. Ex. 28), so the seriousness of the minister's life rests upon him as a vestment. Gregory explained, "The one who is an example for others should always convey, by the seriousness of his life, what a wealth of reason he bears in his breast."[27] In demonstrating virtue, the spiritual director must be "first" in service to others, meaning the main example of service to the congregation so that they can imitate him.[28] He provides a real-life example of what it looks like to walk with God.

Further, in speech, the spiritual director must demonstrate discernment. He must discern what to say and what to refrain from saying, "otherwise he might say something that should have been suppressed or suppress something that should have been said."[29] Speech is indicative of the human heart, so speaking poorly reveals an unwise and potentially unvirtuous soul. Spiritual directors must give just as much consideration to how and when they speak as they do to what they say. Gregory explained,

Spiritual directors must be careful not only to guard against saying something wrong, but also to avoid offering the right

26 Gregory, *Pastoral Rule* 2.1.
27 Gregory, *Pastoral Rule* 2.2.
28 Gregory, *Pastoral Rule* 2.3.
29 Gregory, *Pastoral Rule* 2.4.

words too frequently or unprofessionally, because often the virtue of what is said is lost when it is enfeebled in the hearts of the audience since speech was offered hastily or carelessly. This type of speech defiles the speaker because it shows that he does not know how to serve the advanced needs of his audience.[30]

Hasty speech often does not serve the needs of the community. Pastoral ministry may require the occasional swift response to a pastoral issue, but hurried and superficial language will diminish our ministry to others. Clichés are rarely helpful for true soul care. Thus, Gregory calls us to a quiet and peaceful life, even when we speak to others. We must endeavor to speak more slowly, carefully, and wisely. This does not mean that we are to fear when we speak but simply that we are to give slow and wise consideration to when, how, and what we say.

Conclusion

Overall, emotionally healthy ministers are better equipped for ministry than tired, stressed ones. That health can only come when we prioritize the contemplation necessary to address the matters of our soul. Pete Scazerro drives this point home when he says, "We need to be alone so we can listen."[31] It is in silence and solitude that we can we sincerely listen to our emotions, fears, hopes, and dreams and then place those matters before God in prayer, and this will also allow us to listen to the souls of others. Donald Whitney puts it this way: "Without silence and solitude we can be active, but shallow."[32] Thomas Merton made a similar observation:

30 Gregory, *Pastoral Rule* 2.4.

31 Peter Scazerro, *Emotionally Healthy Spirituality: It's Impossible to be Spiritually Mature While Remaining Emotionally Immature* (Grand Rapids, MI: Zondervan, 2017), 62.

32 Donald S. Whitney, *Spiritual Disciplines for the Christian Life* (Colorado Springs: NavPress, 2014), 225.

There are men dedicated to God whose lives are full of restlessness and have no real desire to be alone. They admit that exterior solitude is good, in theory . . . but in practice, their lives are devoured by activities and strangled with attachments . . . Solitude is impossible for them. They fear it. They do everything they can to escape it. What is worse, they try to draw everyone else into activities as senseless and devouring as their own.[33]

How many pastors struggle with anxieties and worries about their lives, relationships, and the church? We often think that if we work more, we will push the anxiety to the side. But this only exacerbates the problem. We then fear slowing down and don't know how to be alone. We fear silence and, quite possibly, we fear hearing from God. As you begin planning for times of silence and solitude, prepare to meet the chaos that reverberates deep within! But there is much good to be gained from dealing with this chaos. Laird explains, "Silence plays a crucial role in the spiritual life. Environmental silence is the soil in which a healthy contemplative practice takes root."[34] Silence and solitude can lay the fertile ground for your soul to unite more intimately with the triune God. As we lead people to the riches of Christ, may we first be led by the true shepherd of our souls to the quiet, green pasture. May we experience the presence of God anew and receive blessings upon blessings.

33 Thomas Merton, *New Seeds of Contemplation* (New York: New Directions Books, 2007), 83.
34 Martin Laird, *A Sunlight Absence: Silence, Awareness, and Contemplation* (Oxford: Oxford University Press, 2011), 6.

10

The Preaching Pastor and John Chrysostom

What troubles and vexations do you suppose a man endures, if he enters the lists of preaching with [an] ambition for applause? The sea can never be free from waves; no more can his soul be free from cares and sorrow.

JOHN CHRYSOSTOM

I charge you in the presence of God and of Christ Jesus . . . preach the word; be ready in season and out of season; reprove, rebuke, and exhort, with complete patience and teaching.

2 TIMOTHY 4:1–2

IN SEMINARY, I (COLEMAN) remember the excitement I felt when beginning my preaching courses. I was a young minister who was starting to get opportunities to preach and teach in our local church and I was ready to receive more tools to hone my craft. I had taken some introductory courses on pastoral ministry, biblical studies, and systematic theology and was now ready to grow in my skills as an expositor. But after the first few weeks of class, I fell under the crushing weight of what was expected of a preacher. The portrait of a preacher painted for me was of one who spent no less than twenty hours a week in study and preparation. Those who were serious about exegeting the original languages and dealing with different nuances of the text would take even longer. As a young married man, part-time minister, and full-time student, I was more than a little intimated by this description of a good and faithful preacher.

For some pastors, such a schedule may be possible (and occasionally necessary for certain topics), but I have since learned that preaching is best when informed by the weekly duties of pastoral ministry outside the study—sitting next to hospital beds, counseling married couples, and cheering on high schoolers at the local football game—and thus should not be allowed to push those duties aside. Neglect of personal spiritual disciplines and time with others weakens the potential of a weekly sermon.

Thus, we should define pastors as both caretakers of souls and communicators of God's word. First, they are called to handle the word of God with care. It is the "lamp to [our] feet and a light to [our] path" (Ps. 119:105). It is "profitable for teaching, for reproof, for correction, and for training in righteousness, that the man of God may be complete, equipped for every good work" (2 Tim. 3:16–17). It is the sanctifying truth of God (John 17:17). Shepherds are called to "preach the word [and] be ready in season and out of season; reprove, rebuke, and exhort, with complete patience and teaching" (2 Tim. 4:2). Yet, pastors must spend time getting to know God's people in order to make the truth meaningful for their lives. We concur with the great preacher Martyn Lloyd-Jones that the preacher is not merely to influence a part of them; he is not only to influence their minds, or only their emotions, or merely to bring pressure to bear upon their wills and to induce them to some kind of activity. He is there to deal with the whole person; and his preaching is meant to affect the whole person at the very center of life. Preaching should make such a difference to a man who is listening that he is never the same again.[1]

Preaching is a weighty task, but it must be balanced with the other tasks of pastoral ministry, otherwise it will become dry and lifeless. How can this be done? One way to bring the preaching and shepherding tasks of pastoral ministry together is to prepare for the former by meditating on and studying Scripture—translating the text from the original languages and consulting church history if possible—and then opening the church directory and praying for each person who will hear your sermon. In this way, you can prepare a sermon that seeks to inform, transform, and meet the real spiritual needs of your listeners. Let's now look further at why informing, transforming, and meeting needs are three marks of a good sermon, using the church fathers to help us.

Preaching to Inform

In chapter 8 we highlighted the work of Gregory of Nazianzus and his Trinitarian reflection in his *Theological Orations*. This was a monumental work, but it is often forgotten that, rather than being written as a technical treatise, these were sermons given to a real congregation. Their original purpose was to provide the people with vital information about the nature and work of the Father, Son, and

1 D. Martyn Lloyd-Jones, *Preaching and Preachers* (Grand Rapids, MI: Zondervan, 2011), 64.

Spirit so that the congregation could see the beauty of the triune God in the Scriptures. Though these sermons provided more than just information, the *Theological Orations* laid a necessary foundation in theological information for the people who stood in front of Gregory.

Similarly, in chapter 4 we highlighted Origen's groundbreaking work in exegesis and theology that resulted from his hard work in the study, but we must remember that his learning was for the sake of communicating information about the Bible and God to his audience. Andrew Hofer goes so far as to say, "Origen should be ranked as nothing less than pre-Nicene Christianity's most significant preacher after the apostolic era. . . . Origen the consummate teacher preached several hundred homilies because of his great desire for what he considered the goal of preaching: the edification of the Church."[2]

Overall, these two church fathers knew the importance of educating their congregation through preaching and show us that preaching is a task in transmitting crucial information for knowing God, his will, and how he wants us to live. A sermon must first convey the right information before anything else can take place. Preaching that gives false or misleading information can shipwreck God's people on an island of despair and spiritual chaos. But preaching that communicates true spiritual knowledge is a safe and welcoming harbor for storm-tossed souls. Augustine began his treatise on teaching and communicating Scripture, *On Christian Doctrine*, emphasizing this point: "There are two things which all treatment of the scriptures is aiming at: a way to discover what needs to be understood, and a way to put across to others what has been understood."[3] This

2 Andrew Hofer, *The Power of Patristic Preaching: The Word in Our Flesh* (Washington, DC: Catholic University of America Press, 2023), 50–51.

3 Saint Augustine, *Teaching Christianity (De Doctrina Christiana)*, ed. John E. Rotelle, trans. Edmund Hill, The Works of Saint Augustine: A Translation for the 21st Century (Hyde Park, NY: New City, 1996), 1:109.

conviction demonstrated one of the primary roles of the pastor in the early church: to know and communicate God's word to their people. In essence, pastors were communicators of holy knowledge. Christopher Beeley illustrates this point when he says,

> The most immediate and practical means for maintaining a theologically centered leadership is holy scripture. It is through what the Apostle Paul calls the interpretation of scripture "according to the Spirit" that pastors are enabled to be effective guides. The centrality of scripture in the life of faithful church leaders can hardly be exaggerated. . . . For the great leaders of the Christian past holy scripture and the theological perspective it represents stand at the summit of human knowing.[4]

Pastors prioritize their own understanding of Scripture in order to later communicate that to others. But it doesn't so much matter what a particular pastor's level of intelligence or education are—what is most important is a consistent intake and deep study of God's word. Though education is to be valued and sought, "all the fathers insist that whatever training and education one has, what really enables one to teach, delight, and sway others in Christ is a prayerful faith, founded on the spiritual study of scripture."[5] Further, for the church fathers, "Faithfulness, not originality, was the mark of a good teacher."[6] Great preachers have more than rhetorical knowledge—they have a living and active faith connected to their meditation of Scripture. Through the study of Scripture,

4 Christopher A. Beeley, *Leading God's People: Wisdom from the Early Church for Today* (Grand Rapids, MI: Eerdmans, 2012), 81.
5 Beeley, *Leading God's People*, 122.
6 Robert Louis Wilken. *The Spirit of Early Christian Thought: Seeking the Face of God* (New Haven, NJ: Yale University Press, 2003), 27.

ministers are shown what to preach by God himself. Commenting on Psalm 68, Augustine stated,

> Surely the Lord will give his word to [preachers], and so enable them to preach the gospel, only if they sleep in the middle of their allotted inheritances. Only if they are careful not to desert the authority of the two Testaments is the word of truth given to them. If they hold to it, they themselves are the silver wings of the dove, and by their preaching the Church is gloriously borne up to heaven.[7]

Preachers are most effective for God's people when they are most affected by God's word.

Preaching to Transform

Commenting on the type of preaching necessary for a "post-everything" world, Zach Eswine says, "Remove character from content and an inappropriate conservatism emerges. Remove content from character and liberalism surfaces. Preachers must bring to culture the content the Bible presents with the relational character the Bible promotes."[8] According to the fathers, the high calling of pastoral ministry comes with the responsibility of piety.[9] Though this calling was not a rigid moral invective that made imperfection intolerable, it was a call to be a person worthy of imitation. Pastors must exhibit the virtues they wish to see in the lives of their people. Commenting

---

7   Saint Augustine, *Expositions of the Psalms 51–72*, trans. Maria Boulding, ed. John E. Rotelle, The Works of Saint Augustine: A Translation for the 21st Century (Hyde Park, NY: New City, 2001), 17:339.

8   Zack Eswine, *Preaching to a Post-Everything World: Crafting Biblical Sermons That Connect with Our Culture* (Grand Rapids: Baker Books, 2008), 12.

9   This paragraph has been adapted from Coleman Ford, "Let His Manner of Living Be an Eloquent Sermon: Augustine on Pastoral Leadership in De Doctrina Christina (Pt 2)," September 30, 2016, http://www.ancientchristianstudies.com/. Used by permission.

on Ezekiel 34:3–5, Augustine reflected on the effect that pastors can have on their people, saying "Everyone who leads a bad life for all those to see whom he has been put in charge of, as far as he is concerned is killing even the strong ones. Any who imitate him die; whoever doesn't imitate him lives."[10] Beeley explains, "Those who claim that the laity ought to follow what they say but not what they do, so they can lead bad lives and rely on their official authority alone, are not real shepherds, but vicious imposters."[11]

In short, we preach for transformation because preaching aims at the heart in order to stir up Christlikeness in the congregation by the power of God's Spirit. Good preaching is like performing spiritual open-heart surgery on us and our people from the pulpit. Gregory of Nazianzus observed,

> For the guiding of man, the most variable and manifold of creatures, seems to me in very deed to be the art of arts and science of sciences. Anyone may recognize this, by comparing the work of the physician of souls with the treatment of the body; and noticing that, laborious as the latter is, ours is more laborious, and of more consequence, from the nature of its subject matter, the power of its science, and the object of its exercise.[12]

This medical imagery, one that we have discussed already in relation to the office of a minister in general, is also helpful for understanding the specific act of preaching. When ministers prepare

---

10 Saint Augustine, *Sermons 20–50 on the Old Testament*, ed. John E. Rotelle, trans. Edmund Hill, The Works of Saint Augustine: A Translation for the 21st Century (Hyde Park, NY: New City, 1992), 2:307.

11 Beeley, *Leading God's People*, 51.

12 Gregory of Nazianzus, *Oration* 2.16 in *Nicene and Post-Nicene Fathers, Second Series*, vol. 7, trans. Charles Gordon Browne and James Edward Swallow (Peabody, MA: Hendrickson, 1994).

a sermon, they do so with direct and intimate knowledge of his people. This does not mean he knows everything happening to everyone, but it does mean he must preach for ongoing spiritual transformation from God's word. Relationship is vital for communicating virtues and imploring others to lean upon Christ for growth. Peter Sanlon, commenting on the preaching and pastoral ministry of Augustine, notes that

> Augustine's life of preaching, in a context where he offered sacrificial pastoral care, challenges not only those modern preachers who wish to teach while avoiding engagement with people; it calls into question the validity of the academic outlook which prizes detached rational inquiry apart from personal relational encounter. If we really are people with restless hearts, created to dwell together in God's eternal city, it may be that Augustine's preaching in the context of pastoral ministry provides deeper insight about how we learn and flourish than his more famous academic writings.[13]

Sanlon's point can be extended to many church fathers: if you want to know what concerned them most in their ministry, look to their sermons. Wilken thus argues, "The intellectual effort of the early church was at the service of a much loftier goal than giving conceptual form to Christian belief. Its mission was to win the hearts and minds of men and women to change their lives."[14] Supporting spiritual transformation in the congregation should be happening in a variety of ministry contexts, but preaching in particular sets the agenda and reinforces the mission of transformation on a weekly basis.

13 Peter Sanlon, *Augustine's Theology of Preaching* (Minneapolis, MN: Fortress, 2014), xxxi.
14 Wilken, *Spirit of Early Christian Thought*, xiv.

Preaching to Meet Needs

Bryan Chapell rightly argues that

> ultimately, preaching accomplishes its purposes not because of
> the skills or the wisdom of a preacher but because of the power
> of the Scripture proclaimed. Preachers minister with greater zeal,
> confidence, and freedom when they realize that God has taken
> from their backs the monkey of spiritual manipulation. . . . The
> efficacy of the truths in God's message, rather than any virtue
> in the messenger, transforms hearts.[15]

The idea of preaching to meet felt needs is a controversial topic in
homiletics. Felt needs are the needs that the congregation sees as
most relevant to their daily lives. While some of these needs ought
to be addressed in the context of Christian preaching and pastoral
ministry, felt-needs preaching is a slippery slope because it often
puts the people before the text and tends to only address current
issues, not the deeper things of God.

The testimony of early church leaders is that preaching and pastoral ministry are fueled by the Spirit of God working through the
word of God. For them, God's will and revelation were primary.
Yet, the fathers were also sensitive to the needs of their people.
Historian Jaclyn Maxwell notes,

> In many cases, the needs and concerns of ordinary Christians
> shaped the style of sermons, as well as the questions they returned
> to again and again. Because of this element of interaction, it is

possible to observe aspects of the worldviews and daily lives of the preachers' congregations reflected in the subjects and presentation of their sermons.[16]

Further, for many of the fathers, their training in rhetoric allowed them to understand how to persuade people and their training in the Scriptures allowed them to properly direct that persuasion. Though the fathers rejected sophistry as a valid form of communication as it "rewarded delivery, style and ornamentation with little or no attention to substance,"[17] they were trained in oratory skills that helped them identify what their congregations needed to hear in their preaching. In being unafraid of addressing difficult topics, the fathers showed a genuine concern for the deep needs of the souls they preached to. For example, when Basil of Caesarea preached to a wealthy congregation, he unapologetically told them,

You are not disappointed when you must spend gold in exchange in order to purchase a horse. But when you have the opportunity to exchange corruptible things for the Kingdom

---

16 Jaclyn L. Maxwell, *Christianization and Communication in Late Antiquity: John Chrysostom and His Congregation in Antioch* (Cambridge: Cambridge University Press, 2006), 1.

17 Calvin Troup, *Temporality, Eternity, and Wisdom: The Rhetoric of Augustine's Confessions* (Columbia, SC: University of South Carolina Press, 1999), 4. This type of oratory, which allowed the twisting of words and manipulating of hearers, was prevalent in Roman education, and many Christian intellectuals encountered this approach in their training. Macrina the Younger, the older, devout sister of Basil of Caesarea and Gregory of Nyssa, said that Basil would go astray in his life through the accumulation of pride with this type of learning and rhetoric. This is recounted in Macrina's spiritual biography, authored by Gregory of Nyssa, where he observes that Basil was won over to the "ideal of philosophy" so that he renounced worldly attachments and sought after a virtuous Christian life. See Gregory, Bishop of Nyssa, *The Life of Saint Macrina*, trans. Kevin Corrigan (Eugene, OR: Wipf and Stock, 2005), 27.

of Heaven, you shed tears, spurning the one who asks you and refusing to give anything, while contriving a million excuses for your own expenditures.[18]

Similarly, in his sermons on wealth and poverty, Basil exhorted his hearers to take up the cause of the poor by providing for their needs out of the abundance of their wealth. On temporary riches, Basil asserted, "After all, they bring pleasure for only a little while then fade away and disappear, but afterwards a strict accounting of their disbursement will be demanded from you."[19] Basil saw that his audience was too enamored with the vanities of this world and thus preached to the heart to direct his audience's affections toward heavenly things. Today, preachers can follow in the fathers' footsteps by not preaching to felt needs and instead identifying the true spiritual needs of their congregation. They should not tickle ears with worldly wisdom but prick hearts with biblical truth.

John Chrysostom

Surely, this kind of preaching—one that informs, transforms, and addresses real needs—is a weighty task. John Chrysostom (347–407) understood that well and exemplifies how to faithfully preach in one's unique context.

In the fourth century, the emperor Constantine sought to establish a new Rome. The Eastern empire had become increasingly desirable because of its proximity to trade routes and the potential wealth to be gained from its goods, but the Western empire was

---

18 St. Basil the Great, *On Social Justice*, trans. C. Paul Schroeder, Popular Patristics Series 38 (Crestwood, NY: St Vladimir's Seminary Press, 2009), 47.

19 St. Basil the Great, *Homily* 6.2 in *On Social Justice*, trans. C. Paul Schroeder, Popular Patristics Series 38 (Crestwood, NY: St Vladimir's Seminary Press, 2009), 61.

continually subject to Germanic incursions, and Rome, its beacon of light, had lost much of the luster of its former generations because of civil war and urbanization. Constantine wished to erect a city in his image, one that demonstrated his priorities and gave himself the ability to set the agenda for the next phase of Roman imperial dominance. The city that emerged was Constantinople. It was designed with the church in mind and soon became a significant center of ecclesiastical activity.

Of the many who occupied the bishop's throne in Constantinople in the fourth century, Chrysostom is one of the best remembered, both for his force of oratory as well as the controversy it brought him. He first did ministry in Antioch (no small appointment in itself) and then in Constantinople, gaining popularity through his oratory and style of preaching and eventually being called John the Golden Mouth.[20] The Second Nicene Council (787) referred to him as the "father of fathers,"[21] and both the Eastern and Western churches have regarded him as one of the greats for hundreds of years.[22]

Yet, like many other church fathers, Chrysostom was primarily a pastor. In his *On the Priesthood*, he told the story of his call to ministry and discussed the inherent difficulties of the pastoral task. When it came to accepting the call of ministry, Chrysostom

---

20 Two helpful biographies of John Chrysostom are J. N. D. Kelly, *Golden Mouth: The Story of John Chrysostom—Ascetic, Preacher, Bishop* (Ithaca, NY: Cornell University Press, 1995) and Wendy Mayer and Pauline Allen, *John Chrysostom*, Early Church Fathers (London: Routledge, 2000).

21 *Acta*, sixth session, sec. 5 in *The Acts of the Second Council of Nicaea (787)*, vol. 5, trans. Richard Price (Liverpool: Liverpool University Press). See Andrew Louth, "John Chrysostom and the Antiochene School to Theodoret of Cyrrhus," in *The Cambridge History of Early Christian Literature*, ed. Frances Young, Lewis Ayres, and Andrew Louth (Cambridge: Cambridge University Press, 2004), 342–52.

22 Hubertus R. Drobner, *The Fathers of the Church: A Comprehensive Introduction*, trans. Siegfried S. Schatzmann (Peabody, MA: Hendrickson, 2007), 330.

experienced great inner conflict.[23] Echoing Gregory of Nazianzus, Chrysostom said he was afraid of the weighty task of pastoral ministry and the sober reality of caring for souls. He concluded that no one was fit for pastoral ministry and thus all must rely on the grace of God to endure.

In his words, it was "worldly desires" and "youthful vanities" that weighed him down and kept him from pursuing "the true philosophy" of Christianity and monastic living.[24] He described his friend Basil as much more able and willing to enter the ministry. Basil, who was spiritually excelling, remained close to Chrysostom, providing encouragement and accountability. Basil had finally convinced him to pursue a monastic life when Chrysostom's mother intervened. She lamented, "But until I breathe my last, be content to live with me. Do not give needless offence to God by overwhelming me with such misfortunes, for I have never done you any harm."[25] This seems to have convinced Chrysostom to stay and care for his mother and thus postpone his plans until after her passing.

Later, he and Basil caught wind that they were being considered for ordination. Chrysostom recounted his feelings after hearing this news:

For my part, as soon as I heard this story, I was overcome with fear and bewilderment: with fear, that I should be seized against my will, and with bewilderment, as I tried again and again to guess what had induced the men concerned to form such a

23 St. John Chrysostom, *On the Priesthood, Six Books*, trans. Graham Neville, Popular Patristics Series 1 (Crestwood, NY: St Vladimir's Seminary Press, 1977), bk. 3, secs. 6–10.

24 Chrysostom, *On the Priesthood* 1.1.

25 Chrysostom, *On the Priesthood* 1.5.

plan for me. I examined myself and could discover nothing that deserved such an honour.[26]

Chrysostom sought to avoid the calling, if possible, though he was certain his friend Basil was qualified and would be a great service to the church. They agreed to stick together whatever the outcome would be.

Basil eventually pursued this call, thinking Chrysostom had done the same but later discovering that he had been in hiding when the representative from the congregation came to relay the news. The rest of *On the Priesthood* records a dialogue between Chrysostom and Basil on the nature of pastoral ministry that was fueled by Basil's insistence that Chrysostom deceived him when they made a pact to accept the pastoral call together. In his defense, Chrysostom said that many temptations to pride and arrogance resided in the pastoral office and so pride must be dealt with before stepping into the pastorate. He wrote, "If anyone nurtures within himself this terrible, savage beast before attaining office, there is no telling what a furnace he will fling himself into, after he has attained it."[27] Elsewhere he warned his readers to maintain a balance of excellent preaching and humble character, asserting, "What troubles and vexations do you suppose a man endures, if he enters the lists of preaching with this ambition for applause? The sea can never be free from waves; no more can his soul be free from cares and sorrow."[28] Since the temptation to become proud will always remain in pastoral ministry, those considering ministry should begin dealing with any pride that exists in their hearts before entering such ministry.

26 Chrysostom, *On the Priesthood* 1.1.
27 Chrysostom, *On the Priesthood* 1.9.
28 Chrysostom, *On the Priesthood* 1.13.

Chrysostom's reflections run contrary to much contemporary advice for Christian leaders. We're told that through preaching and charisma, leaders ought to impose their will and vision onto the church for the greater good. If someone is not on board, they can get off the bus, either willingly or by force.[29] But while it is true that preachers can wield significant influence over people, we've missed the point if ministry is only for the sake of influence. Chrysostom teaches us that the purpose of preaching is not to accumulate favor or acclaim but to boldly proclaim God's truth. It is a long task of faithfully preaching the text within the community for the sake of forming it more and more into the image of Christ by the power of the Spirit.

Powerful Preaching

Overall, Chrysostom's training in oration and the attention he gave to the needs of his audience made him a powerful preacher. Wendy Mayer and Pauline Allen note, "This preference for directness is characteristic of his preaching in general. The traces of John's rhetorical education can be seen in every aspect of his sermons' structure, content and delivery."[30] However, Chrysostom's preferred audience was the church. During services in the fourth century, bishops normally sat down on the bishop's throne—a stand that was elevated above the congregation—to preach. The bishop's throne was a symbol of the authority of God's word. But Chrysostom wanted to be among the people as he preached, so he stood on the same level as them. Today, this would be the same as a pastor

---

29 This popular understanding of ministry is actually abusive. For example, Mark Driscoll once said there was a "pile of dead bodies behind the Mars Hill bus, and by God's grace, it'll be a mountain by the time we're done." Mike Cosper, "Who Killed Mars Hill?," *Christianity Today*, June 21, 2021, https://www.christianitytoday.com/.

30 Mayer and Allen, *John Chrysostom*, 27.

stepping down from the pulpit to preach on the ground floor. Chrysostom's decision to move locations, however, did not hinder his preaching power but supported it. By moving closer to the congregation, Chrysostom ensured that they could more clearly hear his words. In an age without amplification, he recognized the importance of being in closer proximity to his people. Let's now look at a few examples of this kind of preaching in action—on the topics of wealth, poverty, marriage, and family—to see how Chrysostom wielded his power in order to proclaim the truth.

On Wealth and Poverty

Chrysostom encountered the extremes of absolute wealth and dire poverty when he served as a pastor. Roman society was severely stratified. There was no publicly funded healthcare or welfare system, so those who were not independently wealthy were more susceptible to ruin from illness and ill fortune. It was Christians in the early centuries of the church who stepped in to fill the gap, providing care and resources for the poor.[31] In Constantinople, with the help of a deaconess named Olympia, Chrysostom was able to organize such aid. In Antioch, he estimated that about one-tenth of the population was poor and argued that the church was responsible for caring for those thousands of individuals.[32] Thus, to help his people develop a healthy vision of wealth, Chrysostom preached a series of sermons on the parable of Lazarus and the rich man from

31 In fact, Christians are credited with developing the first hospitals in late antiquity. Though early Christians served the poor and outcast, it was monastic communities in the fourth and fifth centuries that began caring for the physical needs in a more systematic manner. For more on this topic see Andrew Crislip, *From Monastery to Hospital: Christian Monasticism and the Transformation of Health Care in Late Antiquity* (Ann Arbor: University of Michigan Press, 2005).

32 Gary B. Ferngren, *Medicine and Health Care in Early Christianity* (Baltimore: John Hopkins University Press, 2009), 115, 123.

Luke 16. Chrysostom used this parable, which illustrated both the judgment of God and testimony of Christ's resurrection, to reveal the dangers of finding one's identity and comfort in wealth.

Commenting on the fortunes of the rich man, Chrysostom observed, "But that man was not improved by his prosperity, but remained beastly, or rather he surpassed the cruelty and inhumanity of any beast in his behavior."[33] The possession of wealth is not an automatic curse, but it can easily ensnare one's soul. Chrysostom's use of the term "beastly" showed listeners how wealth easily makes one less, rather than more, human.

Chrysostom also described the plight of the rich man as a shipwreck waiting to happen. This man's "cargo" was mean to be offloaded throughout his life, serving the good of others, yet he refused to do so. Chrysostom went so far to state that "there is nothing more grievous than luxury."[34] The pursuit of luxury leads to a life of vice, not virtue. Chrysostom's injunction is worth quoting at length:

> Do not simply tell me of the man who enjoys an expensive table, who wears silken robes, who takes with him flocks of slaves as he struts in the marketplace: unfold for me his conscience, and you will see inside a great tumult of sins, continual fear, storm, confusion, his mind approaching the imperial throne of his conscience as if in a courtroom, sitting like a juror, presenting arguments as if in a public trial, suspending his mind and torturing it for his sins, and crying aloud, with no witness but God who alone knows how to watch these inner dramas.[35]

33 St. John Chrysostom, *On Wealth and Poverty*, trans. Catharine P. Roth, Popular Patristics Series 9 (Crestwood, NY: St Vladimir's Seminary Press, 1981), 22.

34 Chrysostom, *On Wealth and Poverty*, 26.

35 Chrysostom, *De Laz* 1 in *St. John Chrysostom, On Wealth and Poverty*, trans. Catharine P. Roth, Popular Patristics Series 9 (Crestwood, NY: St Vladimir's Seminary Press, 1981), 22.

In other words, the soul that seeks luxury is ultimately at the mercy of fear. The fear of loss, approval, and failing cloud the mind of one seeking wealth as a means of fulfillment. In another sermon on this subject, Chrysostom stated, "So if you see someone greedy for many things, you should consider him the poorest of all, even if he has acquired everyone's money."[36]

Overall, Chrysostom encouraged his listeners to pursue godly virtue above wealth. He unpacked the parable of Luke 16 to show how dangerous wealth can be to the soul. And while poverty alone does not make one virtuous, Chrysostom suggested that the poverty of Lazarus led him to pursue virtue in the face of affliction. Thus Lazarus resides in Abraham's bosom not because he was poor but because he was godly, and the rich man resides in the place of torment not because of his wealth but because of his wickedness. According to Chrysostom, the moral of the story was that if your soul is given over to the vice of luxury, or any vice for that matter, the remedy is always repentance. He asserted, "Nothing is so deadly to sin as self-accusation and self-condemnation with repentance and tears. Have you condemned your sin? Put away the burden."[37] This need for repentance is ongoing, not to appease our conscience or because God is displeased with us, but because we need to be "sober and mindful until the end."[38]

Chrysostom concluded his series of sermons with an exhortation to stay on the narrow road despite its tribulations. The way of worldly comfort, according to Chrysostom, is paved by "the spectacles of Satan" and must be avoided at all costs.[39] The narrow way

36 Chrysostom, *De Laz* 2.
37 Chrysostom, *De Laz* 4.
38 Chrysostom, *De Laz* 4.
39 Chrysostom, *De Laz* 7.

of Christ is what brings the most comfort, including the supreme comfort of eternal life with God. This path is paved with adversity not for adversity's sake but to increase our reliance on God.

Christians today, particularly in the West, are subject to an ever-increasing culture of comfort. Everything seems to cater to maximizing ease and enjoyment while minimizing pain and dissatisfaction. But according to Chrysostom, we are to look to those "ineffable good things which eye has not seen nor ear heard."[40] The treasures we have in Christ, not on earth, are to be our supreme joy and comfort.

On Marriage and Family

Chrysostom also has much wisdom to share with us today regarding marriage and family. Commenting on his homilies on marriage, Catharine Roth says,

> His early life as the son of a widow and as a young monk perhaps failed to give him the opportunity of fully appreciating the potential for grace in married life. Later, his experience as a pastor at Antioch and at Constantinople corrected this imbalance in his understanding, and later he became the great apologist for Christian marriage.[41]

According to David Hunter, Chrysostom encouraged monastic rigor within marriage, particularly around finances, while still maintaining the importance of marital love.[42] Thus, while he elevated

---

40 Chrysostom, *De Laz* 7.

41 Catharine P. Roth, "Introduction," in *On Marriage & Family Life*, John Chrysostom, Popular Patristics Series 7 (Crestwood, NY: St Vladimir's Seminary Press, 1986), 8.

42 David G. Hunter, "Introduction," in *Marriage in the Early Church*, ed. and trans. David G. Hunter (Minneapolis, MN: Fortress, 1992), 20.

the place of virginity in the church, he also recognized that the church was not only a congregation of virgins. Married life was a valid calling for many Christians. John and Stefana Dan Laing note that Chrysostom "proved to be a strong advocate for the goods of marriage, defending it against prominent fourth-century heresies . . . which denigrated marriage and sexual desire."[43] For example, Chrysostom stated,

> There is no influence more powerful than the bond of love, especially for husband and wife. A servant can be taught submission through fear; but even he, if provoked too much, will soon seek his escape. But one's partner for life, the mother of one's children, the source of one's every joy, should never be fettered with fear and threats, but with love and patience. What kind of marriage can there be when the wife is afraid of her husband?[44]

According to Chrysostom, love is one of the most important virtues to express in a marriage but it must be focused in the proper direction. Love of physical things like outward beauty will not sustain a relationship. For married Christians, love should be directed toward a partner's soul. This does not mean that physical attraction is ignored but that it is placed in proper perspective. Soul beauty is the priority of affection in marriage. Thus Chrysostom was able to advocate for chastity even within marriage as "appropriately focused sexual desire and activity."[45]

---

43 John D. Laing and Stefana Dan Laing, " 'To Marry in Christ': A Theological and Ethical Appraisal of John Chrysostom on Marriage," *Journal of the Evangelical Theological Society* 63, no. 1 (March 2020): 142.

44 St. John Chrysostom, *Homily* 20 in *On Marriage & Family Life*, trans. Catharine P. Roth, Popular Patristics Series 7 (Crestwood, NY: St Vladimir's Seminary Press, 1986).

45 Laing and Laing, "To Marry in Christ," 145.

Overall, what Chrysostom calls "true nobility of soul" contrasts with finding one's value in wealth and status, including in marriage.[46] In fourth-century Constantinople, marriage was seen as a means of attaining wealth and security. But Chrysostom found a deeper meaning. He exhorted husbands, "Let us make [wives] fair in God's sight, not in our own."[47] Laing and Laing state,

> Ultimately for Chrysostom, marriage was not politically motivated and not about civic duty. It was spiritual at its core and thoroughly theologically grounded. He believed that when Christian spouses set aside the self and prioritized the other, they exhibited a spiritual love that approximates spiritual birth. . . . [representing] a spiritual birth producing salvation as well as spiritual union with Christ.[48]

Through his preaching, Chrysostom brought his congregation to a more faithful view of marriage as a spiritual good.

In sum, there are three lessons we can take from Chrysostom's preaching on marriage and family. Today, Christians prioritize marriage as the only faithful option for the Christian. Singles in the church are often relegated to a special subset of ministry with the hopes that one day they may finally find someone to complete them. But Chrysostom shows us that some are called to marriage, while others are called to remaining single. This understanding coheres with Paul's instructions in 1 Corinthians 7, and it is clear that the church needs both those who are glorifying God in their marriages and those who are doing this as singles. Both are

46 Chrysostom, *Homily* 20.
47 Chrysostom, *Homily* 20.
48 Laing and Laing, "To Marry in Christ," 158.

a calling from the Lord, and pastors would do well to ensure that their churches do not produce an unhealthy culture by prioritizing one over the other.

Further, when preaching on marriage, pastors need to retain the balances expressed in Scripture. Marriage is neither a place to redeem sexual sin nor seek total life fulfillment. Rather, marriage is good, though certainly fraught with difficulty because of sin, and is, in essence, a laboratory of love, cultivating bonds between spouses and modeling love to children and others. A marriage submerged in fear is not a biblical marriage but an abusive one.

Last, though the power couples in your church may seem to be personally fulfilled and successful, it is important to remember that the real standard for a good marriage is a focus on God's beauty and spiritual growth. Pastors should remind young people considering marriage that this union is primarily concerned with souls, both the wife's and the husband's. Emotional and sexual fulfillment, as well as other benefits of marriage, come about when each spouse cares about the other's life with God.

Conclusion

Overall, Chrysostom preached to inform, transform, and meet the spiritual needs of the church. Using metaphors, similes, imagery, and more, he was able to capture the heart of his audience. Though the power of God's word is not dependent upon "lofty speech or wisdom" (1 Cor. 2:1) and the Spirit is needed to transform hearts, preachers are still called to apply their skill for the purpose of honestly and humbly persuading the people of the truth. Gospel-centered oratory keeps the power of God's word, not the power of human speech, front and center, and it is his word that ultimately fulfills all human longings.

Conclusion

Theology and Ministry
for the Future

AS WE HAVE SEEN, the church fathers are a vast and rich resource of wisdom for pastoral ministry, one that we neglect to our own detriment. Yet, applying the teachings of these sages to our churches is not as simple as occasionally plopping a short quote into our sermons. We must take time to mine the depths of Christian antiquity, be shaped by its world, and consider the theological riches of our heritage before we can begin reshaping our present landscape. We become different kinds of thinkers, even different kinds of people, when we meet our ancient fathers face-to-face and then bring the fruits of these encounters to our ministry. And we must not forget that they themselves forged theology in the life and context of the church. When we read about Augustine's spiritual life, we must remember that he wrote about his personal experiences in the church. When we read about Athanasius's theological vision, we must remember that he served as a bishop. When we read about Gregory of Nazianzus's Trinitarianism, we must remember that he shared his most influential ideas in sermons. For the fathers, theology was not theoretical speculation; it was an act of worship.

Lessons from the Classical Tradition

In this book, we attempted not to address every issue that pastors face today but to reflect on ministry alongside the fathers. Overall, they have showed us that the pastoral calling not only permits but even requires a pastor to contemplate God and care for souls. Christ is the ultimate cure for sick souls, and pastors must know how to apply such cure to each unique person in order to treat spiritual ailments. Augustine said, "Just as physicians when they bind up wounds do not do so haphazardly but neatly so that a certain beauty accompanies the utility of the bandages, so the medicine of Wisdom by taking on humanity is accommodated to our wounds, healing some by contraries and some by similar things."[1] We have learned much by listening to the fathers. Let's reflect on some unifying themes that we first mentioned in our introduction and have now seen up close in subsequent chapters:

(1) Classical theology. Theological depth and clarity are needed for the health of the church. As noted throughout this book, the fathers integrated their keen understanding of the Bible and theology in order to weave every strand of Scripture together with the thread of Christ. Theologian Kathryn Tanner observes,

> The whole of who God is for us as creator and redeemer, which in its varied complexity might simply overwhelm and mystify us, is found in concentrated compass in Christ. Christ in this way

---

1   Saint Augustine, *Teaching Christianity (De Doctrina Christiana)*, ed. John E. Rotelle, trans. Edmund Hill, The Works of Saint Augustine: A Translation for the 21st Century (Hyde Park, NY: New City, 1996), bk. 1, chap. 14, sec. 13.

provides . . . a clue to the pattern or structure that organizes the whole even while God's ways remain ultimately beyond our grasp.[2]

The fathers clearly demonstrated this thought pattern. Growing in theological depth may be a slow process, but it always bears fruit for the church.

(2) Virtue. Virtue and the life of the pastor belong together. Ethics and spiritual formation are essential components of ministerial training. Pastors cannot separate who they are from what they do. And though they are never perfect, they set the standard of holy living in the local church. Thus, morality is not tangential to but inherent in the pastoral call. Voices such as Gregory of Nazianzus, John Chrysostom, and Augustine told us of the high moral summons of pastoral life. Overall, recovering this essential element of virtue will lead to healthier pastors and more faithful congregants.

(3) Integrated spirituality and theology. This has two implications. First, it means that high-level theology is meant to serve the church. Each time we (Coleman and Shawn) read a patristic volume, we realize that we are probably reading a book written by a pastor. Next time you pick up a patristic text, pay attention to the introductory material. For example, Origen wrote *Contra Celsum* because one of his pupils asked for a response to the philosopher Celsus, who denied the virgin birth. Further, Basil of Caesarea addressed *On the Holy Spirit* to Bishop Amphilocius and Gregory the Great addressed *Pastoral Rule* to a fellow pastor named John.

Theology is not just for the academy. In fact, it is primarily for the church. Thus, pastors and ministry leaders must clear a way for their congregations to understand high-level theology by first studying

2   Kathryn Tanner, *Christ the Key*, Current Issues in Theology (Cambridge: Cambridge University Press, 2010), viii.

it themselves and then clarifying theological issues for their people. They need good theology sourced from Scripture and tradition, and pastors serve as the resident theologians who will give this to them.

Second, this means that asceticism, contemplation, and spirituality tether a minister to the divine life of God. Busy pastors and ministry leaders must stop, be still, and contemplate God more. Both the academic pastor and outgoing pastor should not let study or activity keep them from tending to their spiritual needs or spending quiet time with God. Contemplation and the ascent of the soul must occupy the minister's attention on a regular basis in order to operate from dependence on God instead of self-sufficiency. Gregory of Nyssa showed us the importance of contemplating God, Gregory the Great exemplified a life that moved between contemplation and ministerial engagement, and Augustine's cartography of the soul taught us how the inner life relates to God. Overall, their lives demonstrate that contemplating God is a way of life, and ministry flows from this way of life.

(4) Local community. Though the fathers convened at local and global councils, they first and foremost performed ministry in their own churches and cities. Ambrose *of Milan*, Augustine *of Hippo*, and Cyril *of Alexandria* were tied to cities and churches in those cities. Their homilies and tracts were written from and for a local setting. Sermons outside their home church were the exception, not the rule. Thus, the pastor's goal should not be to write the next bestseller or become a highly sought after conference speaker but to know and be known by his local church and community. If he becomes famous through writing or speaking, it ought to fuel his ministry in the local church, not take away from it.

(5) Care of souls. Pastoral ministry is soul care. Caring for your soul and the souls connected to you is the essence of this artful task.

It is unpredictable and requires you to move quickly on your feet, respond to an endless variety of issues, dig into your study, minister to diverse individuals, and contemplate God. Like a small-town doctor on call, pastors stand ready to administer spiritual therapies for sick and weary souls.

Practical Ways to Implement These Lessons

So how can we put all of this into practice? Here some practical steps you can take to follow the example of the church fathers as described above:

- Clarify your work duties in order to simplify your schedule. You may need to converse with staff members, elders, deacons, or your denomination to make sure you are on the same page.
- Read the church fathers (see our list of suggested readings at the back of this book for places to start).
- Study Greek and Hebrew. If you never learned these languages, there are many print and online resources—not to mention seminary classes—that can teach you.
- Love God through contemplation, prayer, and theological study. To do this you must make time for intentional devotion to God and come to him with a posture of humility.
- Love your neighbor through soul care, discipleship, and clear preaching in the local church. By focusing on these basics, you demonstrate to your people that the Christian life is simultaneously ordinary and world-shaking.

We (Coleman and Shawn) are not perfect pastors, and we suspect you aren't either. All ministry leaders are being sanctified. All of us have gaps, and by God's grace, those gaps are being revealed and filled by the Lord. Only God through the work of his Spirit can transform us into ministry leaders who look and act more like Jesus.

Our desire and our hope is for you to know how essential your work is to the spiritual growth of your people. You are not alone because there have been many pastors before you, practicing the same art. You are not alone because we are here to encourage you while standing on the shoulders of those we've discussed in this book. The church has labored to clarify her theological identity and the Spirit has guided her. Seek to build on this heritage of soul care, which is truly the art of arts.

Suggested Reading

Primary Sources

Saint Athanasius the Great. *On the Council of Nicaea (De Decretis)*. In *Athanasius*. Translated by Khaled Anatolios.. London: Routledge, 2004.

———. *On the Incarnation*. Translated by John Behr. Popular Patristics Series 44a. Yonkers, NY: St Vladimir's Seminary Press, 2011.

Augustine. *Confessions*. Translated by Henry Chadwick, Oxford World's Classics. Oxford: Oxford University Press, 1998.

———. *Teaching Christianity (De Doctrina Christiana)*. Edited by John E. Rotelle. Translated by Edmund Hill. The Works of Saint Augustine: A Translation for the 21st Century. Hyde Park, NY: New City, 1996.

St. Basil the Great. *On the Holy Spirit*. Translated by Stephen M. Hildebrand. Popular Patristics Series 42. Yonkers, NY: St. Vladimir's Seminary Press, 2011.

———. *Homily* 20. In *On Christian Doctrine and Practice*. Popular Patristics Series 47. Yonkers, NY: St. Vladimir's Seminary Press, 2012.

Chadwick, Henry trans. *Origen: Contra Celsum*. London: Cambridge University Press, 1953.

"Chalcedon Definition." In *The Acts of the Council of Chalcedon: Translated with an Introduction and Notes*, 2:204. Translated Texts for Historians 45. Liverpool: Liverpool University Press, 2005.

Corrigan, Kevin, trans. *Gregory, Bishop of Nyssa: The Life of Saint Macrina.* Eugene, OR: Wipf and Stock, 2005.

DelCogliano, Mark trans., "Augustine of Hippo, *Sermon 52.*' In Andrew Radde-Gallwitz, ed. *God: The Cambridge Edition of Early Christian Writings*, vol. 1. Cambridge: Cambridge University Press, 2017.

Didache. In *The Apostolic Fathers: Greek Texts and English Translations.* Edited by Michael W. Holmes. 3rd ed. Grand Rapids: Baker Academic, 2007.

St. Gregory the Great. *The Book of Pastoral Rule.* Translated by George E. Demacopoulos. Popular Patristics Series 34. Crestwood, NY: St. Vladimir's Seminary Press, 2007.

St. Gregory of Nazianzus. *Theological Orations.* In *On God and Christ: The Five Theological Orations and Two Letters to Cledonius.* Translated by Frederick Williams and Lionel Wickham. Popular Patristics Series 23. Crestwood, NY: St Vladimir's Seminary Press, 2002.

Gregory of Nyssa. *Gregory of Nyssa: The Life of Moses.* Translated by Abraham J. Malherbe and Everett Ferguson. The Classics of Western Spirituality. New York: Paulist, 1978.

Hill, Edmund and John E. Rotelle, ed. *Saint Augustine: The Trinity.* The Works of Saint Augustine, 2nd ed. Hyde Park, NY: New City Press, 2015.

Pelikan, Jaroslav and Valerie Hotchkiss, eds. "Apostles' Creed." In *Creeds & Confessions of Faith in the Christian Tradition*, 1:667–69. New Haven, CT: Yale University Press, 2003.

———. "Athanasian Creed." In *Creeds & Confessions of Faith in the Christian Tradition*, 1:673–77. New Haven, CT: Yale University Press, 2003.

———. "Constantinople Creed." In *Creeds & Confessions of Faith in the Christian Tradition*, 1:160–63. New Haven, CT: Yale University Press, 2003.

———. "Nicene Creed." In *Creeds & Confessions of Faith in the Christian Tradition*, 1:156–59. New Haven, CT: Yale University Press, 2003.

Secondary Sources

Anatolios, Khaled. *Retrieving Nicaea: The Development and Meaning of Trinitarian Doctrine.* Grand Rapids, MI: Baker Academic, 2011.

Ayres, Lewis. *Augustine and the Trinity.* Cambridge: Cambridge University Press, 2010.

———. *Nicaea and its Legacy: An Approach to Fourth-Century Trinitarian Theology.* Oxford: Oxford University Press, 2004.

Barnes, Michel René. "The Fourth Century as Trinitarian Canon." In *Christian Origins: Theology, Rhetoric, and Community*, 47–67. Edited by Lewis Ayres and Gareth Jones. London: Routledge, 1998.

Behr, John. *The Way to Nicaea. Formation of Christian Theology.* Crestwood, NY: St. Vladimir's Seminary Press, 2001.

———. *The Nicene Faith: Part 1 & Part 2.* Formation of Christian Theology. Crestwood, NY: St. Vladimir's Seminary Press, 2001.

Casiday, Augustine, and Frederick W. Norris, eds. *The Cambridge History of Christianity: Constantine to c. 600.* Cambridge, UK: Cambridge University Press, 2007.

Eastman, David L. *Early North African Christianity: Turning Points in the Development of the Church.* Grand Rapids, MI: Baker Academic, 2021.

Fairbairn, Donald. *Life in the Trinity: An Introduction to Theology with the Help of the Church Fathers*. Downers Grove, IL: IVP Academic, 2009.

Ferguson, Everett. *Baptism in the Early Church: History, Theology, and Liturgy in the First Five Centuries*. Grand Rapids, MI: Eerdmans, 2013.

Hall, Christopher A. *Living Wisely with the Church Fathers*. Downers Grove, IL: IVP Academic, 2017.

Haykin, Michael A. G. *Giving Glory to the Consubstantial Trinity: An Essay on the Quintessence of the Christian Faith*. Greenbrier, AR: Free Grace, 2018.

———. *Rediscovering the Church Fathers: Who They Were and How They Shaped the Church*. Wheaton, IL: Crossway, 2011.

Haykin, Michael A. G., and Shawn J. Wilhite, ed. *Early Church Fathers*. 6 vols. Christian Focus.

McGowan, Andrew B. *Ancient Christian Worship: Early Church Practices in Social, Historical, and Theological Perspective*. Grand Rapids, MI: Baker Academic, 2014.

O'Keefe, John J., and R. R. Reno. *Sanctified Vision: An Introduction to Early Christian Interpretation of the Bible*. Baltimore, MD: Johns Hopkins University Press, 2005.

Toom, Tarmo. *Classical Trinitarian Theology: A Textbook*. London: T&T Clark, 2007.

Wilken, Robert Louis. *The Spirit of Early Christian Thought: Seeking the Face of God*. New Haven, CT: Yale University Press, 2005.

Williams, Rowan. *Arius: Heresy & Tradition*. Grand Rapids, MI: Eerdmans, 2001.

General Index

Aaron, 192
Aeneid (Virgil), 143–44
Against Heresies (Irenaeus of Lyons), 101–2, 105–6
Agapetus, Pope, 187
Alexander, 118, 123
Alexandria, 87
Alypius of Thagaste, 148, 152, 153
ambition, 20, 31
Ambrose of Milan, 14, 51–53, 57–69, 70–71, 77, 90–91, 147, 220
Amphilocius, 165, 219
anti-intellectualism, 74, 156, 157
Antoninus, 92
Antony, 127–28, 130
Apology for his Flight to Pontus and On the Priesthood (Gregory of Nazianzus), 165–66
Apostles' Creed, 7
Apostolic Teaching (Irenaeus of Lyons), 111
Aquila, 92, 93
Arianism, 123
Arius of Alexandria, 118, 123, 173
asceticism, 40, 220
Athanasian Creed, 7
Athanasius of Alexandria, 117–19, 123–27, 130–35, 217

Augustine of Hippo, 14, 21–22, 37, 91, 127, 137, 139, 141–53, 188, 198–201, 217, 219, 220
Aurelius, Marcus, 143
authenticity, 113–14
Auxentius, 57

baptism, 35, 52, 53–57, 60–62, 64
Basil of Caesarea, 19, 22–24, 26–27, 29, 77, 165, 166, 204–5, 207–8, 219
Bavinck, Herman, 175
Bible, 77, 77n4, 98–99, 100, 111, 162–64
Bonhoeffer, Dietrich, 185
Book on Pastoral Rules (Gregory the Great), 188–89
Brainerd, David, 186

Carterios, 165
Chalcedonian Definition, 7
Christ-centeredness, 119–23, 127–30, 163
Christianity, 109, 112, 129, 132, 187, 198, 207
Christian life, 54, 66–68, 98, 109, 119, 121, 129, 134, 156
Christians, 3, 4, 26, 38, 42–49, 69–70, 74, 79, 89, 101, 113–15, 127, 144, 183, 210n31, 213–15
  professing Christians, 54

Scripture Index